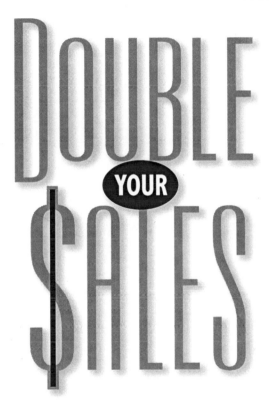

DOUBLE YOUR $ALES

YOUR

An Honest and Authentic
Approach to Professional Selling

BY SCOTT FARNSWORTH

ISBN 0-9719177-9-5

Copyright © 2009 by Scott M. Farnsworth

Cover and Interior Design by Julie Hoyt Dorman, Dorman Graphics, DormanGraphics.com

Published by SunBridge, Inc.
3214 Bayflower Avenue
Harmony, Florida
United States of Ameria
Phone 407-593-2386
Fax 407-292-6242
www.DoubleYourSalesNow.com

Table of Contents

Foreword

By Bradley L. Hahn, Esq.

I figured when I graduated from law school I would never have to sell.

I had no previous sales training and I thought my newly-minted JD gave me an "out." In my mind, selling had no part in one of the "learned professions," and besides, I reasoned, I wouldn't need to sell anyway because clients would simply hire me because I was a lawyer.

Boy, was I wrong!

I struggled mightily to build my estate planning practice for many years. I was never short of qualified prospects, even early in my career, thanks to my youthful energy and lots of wonderful referral sources. But even with a steady stream of prospects, I couldn't seem to "close the deal" often enough to reach my revenue targets.

My initial meetings with prospects were awkward and ineffective. I had no track to run on so I just said whatever popped into my head. I had no clue what prospects were thinking, so when it came time to quote a fee and ask for the business, I was shooting in the dark. Most of the time I totally missed the mark.

After striking out dozens of times, I surmised I was losing business because I didn't know enough about the law. "No problem," I thought, "I can fix that." I spent a pile of money and thousands of hours on continuing legal education—"CLE" it's called in the business—studying everything that remotely resembled my area of practice.

Unfortunately, all that CLE didn't help me get new clients. In fact, it seemed to make things worse. The more I talked about how I could fix their problems with all the new techniques I'd learned at CLE courses, the more my prospects seemed overwhelmed by all the technical information and turned off about working with me.

Then in 2000, a trusted friend who knew my frustrations told me he wanted to introduce me to Scott Farnsworth. He told me he thought Scott's professional sales training course could help me solve this vexing problem.

But being a well-trained attorney, I was wary and seriously skeptical. I still resisted the whole idea of "selling" and especially resented the notion that I needed "sales training." After all, I was a professional, and professionals are above selling, and besides, I had already attended enough courses to last a lifetime. To his credit, my friend stuck to his guns and insisted that I at least talk to Scott, and I agreed to that.

That first call with Scott was very engaging, and by the end of it I agreed to come to the program. I knew I needed help, and Scott helped me see that if I kept doing what I had always done, I would keep getting the results I had always gotten. He explained his approach to me and shared results from others who had attended the course. It started to make sense.

Looking back, I now realize that Scott was simply practicing what he preached—he used the Double Your Sales process to help me decide to help myself. I'm sure glad he did, because his professional selling course turned my business around almost at once.

I learned in Scott's course that the Double Your Sales approach is based on genuinely caring for and connecting with people. I learned about the power of story and how to harness that energy to understand prospective clients more readily and to communicate with them more effectively. I learned how to help them appreciate the serious dangers they face so they can more easily see the value of the solutions I offer.

Most importantly, I learned how to be myself, open my heart to people, and speak in my own authentic voice in initial client meetings. That has made all the difference.

I went from skeptic to convert in two short days. Notwithstanding the rough and ragged way I initially used the process, I had immediate success. I engaged the first 18 prospective client families in a row following Scott's training, and all paid me substantial fees. My sales didn't double; they quadrupled. It was easy and really boosted my confidence.

Since then, it's only gotten better. I seldom miss a sale, and I've been hired for some of the largest fee cases around. Now that I know the right way to conduct an initial meeting with prospective clients, I don't mind selling a bit.

Who says you can't teach an old lawyer new tricks?

—*Bradley L. Hahn, Esq.*
Bradley L. Hahn PC
Legacy Innovation, Inc.
Tempe, Arizona

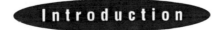

Simple and Obvious

This is a simple and straightforward book about a practical and straightforward process for turning more prospects into paying customers—customers who buy more, buy more often, and at higher prices.

One of my clients, an agent for a large insurance company, made this observation after being taught this process and applying it in his work. "Some of the most effective parts," he said, "are stupidly simple and 'duh' obvious. But," he went on, "it gets results with real customers. I love it because it's simple, it's obvious, and it works."

According to one account, several years after his historic discoveries, Christopher Columbus was invited to a banquet where he was treated like royalty. By then, trips from Spain to the Americas had become commonplace. A shallow courtier, deeply jealous of the great Admiral, sought to embarrass him by asking loudly whether, had he not discovered the West Indies, there were not many other men in Spain who would have been capable of the same thing. After all, the whole concept of sailing west to reach east was so simple and obvious.

Columbus did not reply directly but instead took a raw egg and invited the company to make it stand on end. They all attempted it, but in vain. He then picked up the egg and tapped it lightly on the large end so as to indent the shell only slightly. Without a word, he left the egg standing on the indentation. Once he had shown the way, it was easy.

Similarly, this approach to professional selling is built on principles and insights that, once unveiled, may appear simple and obvious. But don't be misled by the simplicity of these ideas. To underestimate their power and effectiveness because of their simplicity would be a serious mistake.

I have chosen to present this process in a practical and unpretentious manner, free of fancy theories and fanfare. My purpose in writing is not to dazzle you. My purpose is to make it easy for you to grasp the basic concepts that underpin this amazing approach and to master the key stories that make up this potent process. With those under your belt, you'll be on your way to greater sales in almost no time.

May you find success and satisfaction as you learn to Double Your Sales with this honest and authentic approach to professional selling. It's simple, it's obvious, and it works!

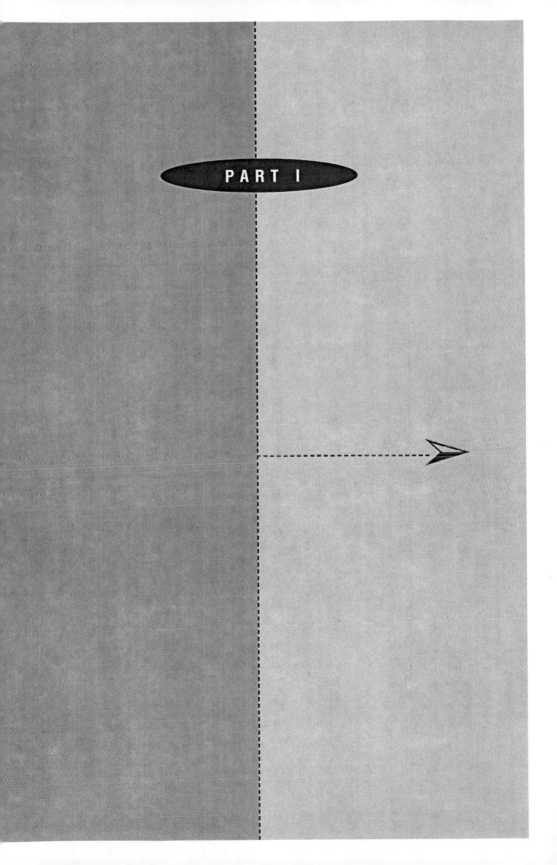

PART I

Chapter 1

John's Dilemma

John loved his business but he hated his job. Actually, what he hated was the business side of his job. No, to be honest, what he really hated was the selling part of his job. And because of that, he was frustrated, personally and financially. ➤

John loved his business because it allowed him to help great people do important things. John was a philanthropy advisor. He helped affluent families figure out how they most wanted to make a difference in the world, and then he designed charitable giving strategies that meshed his clients' philanthropic goals with federal and state tax laws and with the needs of worthy charities.

People who understood John's business told him he offered an extremely valuable set of services, something that was sorely needed. His clients loved him and gave him lavish praise, and the charities he worked with were very pleased with his work. They steered lots of prospects his way, as did other professionals in his area. John was seeing plenty of potential clients; he just couldn't seem to turn them into paying clients. They said they couldn't see the point of paying his fees.

John offered a wonderful service. He knew his stuff. He gave·his clients excellent care. He had an outstanding reputation. He was a great marketer. He had a steady flow of qualified prospects. He just couldn't sell.

His financial frustration at work was bleeding over into his home life. He tried not to take his money worries home, but his wife was no dummy. She knew their family was creeping closer and closer to the financial edge. But she also knew that John didn't need more pressure from her; he needed confidence in himself and his ability to sell.

John had known for a long time he was lousy at sales, but he couldn't figure out what to do about it. At first, like the lyrics to that old Paul Simon song, John decided "the problem is all inside your head." He just needed a more positive mental attitude. He just needed to psych himself up more before sales meetings. He just needed a few convincing "I'm a great salesman!" affirmations to recite to himself while shaving and driving to work.

He tried it, and for a time, it seemed to help. But as soon as the novelty wore off, reality set in. John soon realized that a positive attitude, psyching up, and a whole commute's worth of affirmations weren't going to improve his selling skills. His frustration mounted.

It occurred to John that he'd never been taught how to sell. That subject wasn't covered in college or anywhere in his professional training. "Maybe there's a course that could help me," he thought. But the ideas of a sales training course made John nervous.

John had gone to some "sales training" sessions at professional conferences he attended, and what he heard there made him pretty uncomfortable. Their approaches all seemed based on shading the truth, creating artificial pressure, and even manipulating prospects. Even if those techniques worked, he couldn't do that. It just felt so phony.

But as his desperation grew his resolve to steer clear of those approaches weakened. "I have to get real," he told himself. "I can sit here on my high horse and my family will starve to death, or I can get down and dirty and make enough money to pay the mortgage."

He asked some of his professional colleagues if they had any recommendations. One of them, a life insurance and annuities professional, told John about a sales training course he had attended. He said it was the best thing out there and probably the closest to what John was looking for.

John checked out the course's web site, which promised remarkable results with minimal effort. The cost of the course plus travel expenses was pretty high, but John reasoned that if it increased his sales, it would be worth it. "Maybe it can work for me," John thought. He had to do something, anything. He talked it over with his wife, crossed his fingers, and registered for the course.

John realized in the first thirty minutes of the workshop that he'd made a mistake, a big, expensive mistake. He knew he could never implement their "program;" it just didn't fit who he was. He knew he could never talk to people and treat people the way they were teaching.

He shared his feelings with his wife that night on the phone. She said she understood, but encouraged him to stay for the second day and try to get something worthwhile out of the course. After all, she reminded him, he'd already paid for it and couldn't get his money back.

The next day was miserable for John. The more he heard of their "program," the more it grated on him. And if this was the best out there, now what was he going to do? The plane ride home was nearly unbearable. Hope was fading fast . . . .

[To be continued.]

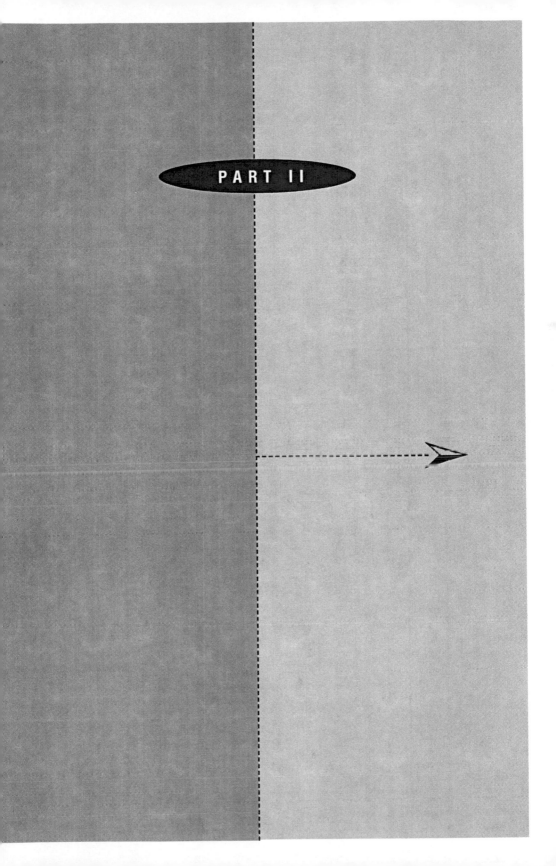

PART II

Chapter 2

Three Simple Secrets

Key Points

➤ If you develop friendships with prospective customers, they will *buy* from you and they will buy *more* from you.

➤ The secret to strong and lasting friendships is creating and nourishing credible stories of a shared future.

➤ It's easy to develop friendships with prospective customers once you understand how stories work.

Who Make the Best Customers?

This is a book about relational selling, and it's based on three of life's simplest yet most valuable secrets. Credit Abraham Lincoln with stating the obvious. He said, "If you can't make a living from your friends, you surely can't make one from your enemies." Or to put it another way, friends make the best customers. The first of the three simple secrets is something you learned with your earliest lemonade stand or paper route:

1] Friendship turns prospects into customers.

If you can develop meaningful relationships with prospective customers, they will *buy* from you and they will buy *more* from you. If you can't, they will buy from you only if they have to, and they will buy as little from you as they can.

What is a Friend?

If friends make the best customers, what then is a friend? With whom can you say you have a meaningful relationship? While some would argue that it's someone with whom you share a past, I believe it's someone with whom you share a future.

Our lives are full of "ex's" and "former's" and "used-to-be's." We share memories with them, but memories don't equal friendships. We may share a past with them, but if we can't look ahead and see our lives somehow intertwined in a positive way, there's no real friendship.

A friend is someone with whom you share a credible story of a mutual future. Here's the second secret:

2] You make friends by creating a positive story of your future together.

So how do you make a friend? You make a friend by fostering with another person a story of your future together.

If you want to develop a relationship today, you must develop a shared vision of tomorrow. Strong and lasting relationships belong to those who can create and nourish future mutual stories with others.

With a shared future story, friendships will emerge even in the harshest environment. Without a credible story of a future together, they won't, regardless of what other conditions are present. A shared vision of your tomorrow is the *sine qua non* of every meaningful friendship today.

Want proof? Just evaluate any "friendship" from any facet of your life by answering frankly these questions:

- Do you share a vision of your future together?
- Does your story harmonize with theirs?
- Does your story continue to inspire you both?

In your honest answers, you can see that the quality of any friendship is never better than the quality of the story of your future together. Real relationships are based on a shared future story. It's as simple as that.

How Do You Develop or Revive a Friendship?

Now here's the best news of all. Once you understand how stories work, you'll realize that it's pretty easy to develop a new relationship or revive an old one. All you have to do is create and nourish the story of your mutual future. Here's the third secret:

3] The process of developing a friendship based on story is simple and easy to learn.

The purpose of this book is to teach you how to do that comfortably, consistently, and confidently in conversations with prospective customers. The art of creating a credible story of a future together is something you can master quickly, easily, and authentically.

How Can You Use This Understanding?

You can use these insights in lots of ways, both personally and professionally. You can strengthen your marriage by rejuvenating the story of your future together. You can fortify your bond with your children, your parents, or your siblings by focusing on what you both want for your mutual tomorrows. You can mend a rift with a neighbor, with a co-worker, or with someone in your church. You can "excuse yourself" from a phony or toxic relationship because you recognize that it has no future.

Knowing these secrets will make you more perceptive about relationships in many settings. If you understand these principles, you can easily explain the existence or non-existence of long-term relationships everywhere and in every realm: in sales, in employment, in politics, in parenting, in the PTA.

With these secrets in mind, you will recognize that without a credible story of a future together, all interactions—whether "one and done" or a string or series—are transactional, not relational. Two people or two groups of people may occupy the same space, be it a home, an office, a business, a community, a political party, or a country, but without the presence of a shared future story, they are just cohabitating; they are not in a meaningful relationship.

These three simple secrets can turn your business around quickly. Once you recognize that friendships are the key to selling, once you understand that friendships arise from creating a future story together, and once you appreciate that creating a future story together is a skill you can learn easily and naturally, you'll start seeing results at once. You'll be able to double your sales in practically no time.

The key is understanding how stories work and how the two sides of our brains work, and then putting that understanding to work with prospective customers. That's the subject of Chapters 3 and 4.

Chapter Summary

- Customers will buy from you and they will buy more from you if you are friends with them.

- Friendships can exist only if people are able to create a credible and compelling story of their future together.

- A shared future story is the *sine qua non* of every meaningful and ongoing friendship.

- You can create or revive a friendship by focusing on developing a shared future story.

- Mastering the art of fostering a shared future story with prospective customers is a skill you can learn quickly, once you understand how stories work.

Chapter 3

How Stories Work

Key Points

➤ Story is our native language. It is the water we swim in. Thus, the best way to communicate with prospective customers is usually through a story.

➤ Stories affect us differently, as expressed in this quote:

Tell me a fact and I'll learn.
Tell me a truth and I'll believe.
Tell me a story and it will live in my heart forever.

—*Steve Sabo*

➤ In the Double Your Sales approach, stories are part of a graceful and elegant interaction. This approach is a dance, not a march; it's a conversation, not a sparring match.

Story is the Best Way to Communicate

If the secret to sales is relationships, and if the key to relationships is stories, then it follows that to get better at sales, you need to get better at stories. To do that, it helps to have a deeper understanding of how stories work.

The first sentence of *The Leader's Guide to Storytelling*, Stephen Denning's groundbreaking book about using stories in business leadership, states: "This book is an account of a simple but powerful idea: the best way to communicate with the people you are trying to lead is very often through a story."

My message is similar. **The best way to communicate with prospective customers is very often through a story. Or to be more precise, through a sequence of stories.**

Story is our Native Language.

One of the reasons this is true is because story is our native language. Until we were a dozen or so years old, it was how we figured out what was going on around us. It was how our parents taught us right from wrong. It was how we played: cops and robbers, cowboys and Indians, Barbie and Ken. It was how we learned and made sense of the world. The language of story was how we connected and communicated with those around us.

It wasn't until later that we learned to be analytical, and even much later that much of our native expression in story was replaced with numbers, analysis, and techno-speak. But a part of us still longs for story, this most human of media.

I have had some interesting experiences that helped me appreciate the importance of communicating in our "common native language." One of my college degrees is in Portuguese, which I earned after I had spent a number of years in Brazil speaking mostly Portuguese. Unfortunately, I subsequently lived for 20 years in places where no other person spoke Portuguese; consequently I lost the ability to speak comfortably in this second language.

Now I live in the Orlando, Florida, area and have frequent opportunities to speak Portuguese. But because of that 20-year hiatus, I have to work hard to be fully present in the conversation. I notice how tense I become as I struggle to remember how to express a certain thought or conjugate a particular verb, or construct agreement between nouns and adjectives. I'm sure I often miss the meanings of the other person's statements, and certainly the nuances of tone and expression.

Occasionally the person I'm speaking with, recognizing that their English is better than my Portuguese, will switch the conversation from Portuguese to English. It's amazing to me to notice how I immediately relax, begin to enjoy the exchange of ideas, and grasp the whole conversation.

Similarly, I've discovered in meetings with clients in professional settings that if I change from the typical language of the profession into the client's native language of story, the whole tone of the conversation changes. They relax, they enjoy the exchange of ideas, and they grasp more of what I'm seeking to share with them. More importantly, they begin to open up and share who they are with me.

Stories Help Us Handle Lots of Information

Creating stories is one of the ways our brains cope with an otherwise unmanageable supply of information. Our brains could not absorb the full range of sensory, mental, and emotional input that floods into them without some sort of artificial construct to help them create a frame of reference. In order to handle the load, our brains reorganize much of this vast amount of sensory, mental, and emotional information into story.

The core of the human mind is a storyteller. Because stories allow us to assemble vast amounts of information in our brains, we are able to retain it, organize it, apply it, and recall it. This allows us to function more effectively in the world.

Our Stories Make Us Who We Are

Over time, these stories become the reality we live in, much as water is the medium fish swim in. Our lives are based not so much on what has happened to us, but on the stories we tell about what has happened to us.

This is evidenced by listening to two people who have survived a common traumatic episode. One of them may say, "Oh, what a terrible experience! My life will never be the same. It has ruined everything." The other, having experienced the very same event, may say, "Yes, it was terrible, but just look how blessed I am to have come out of it alive and how much I learned in the process." Two people who share the same event and have common experiences end up with very different stories.

Added together, these story-experiences constitute the themes of our lives. Over time, who we are becomes inseparable from the stories we tell about who we are. Chinua Achebe has written: "We create stories and stories then create us. It is a rondo." Clarissa Pinkola Estes said it this way: "The stories have grown the storytellers, grown them into who they are."

Stories Affect Us Differently Than Other Communication

There's something different about the way a story touches us and inspires us and moves us to take action, compared to other ways of communicating. Steve Sabo captured the essence of this difference when he stated:

- Tell me a fact and I'll learn.
- Tell me a truth and I'll believe.
- Tell me a story and it will live in my heart forever.

As a professional advisor, as well as in my roles as a father, grandfather, teacher, and citizen, I want the things I say to live in my listeners' hearts and hopefully change their lives in positive ways. So along with all the other ways I might express myself, I need to be sure that I use lots of stories.

It is not altogether clear why stories have such impact, but I believe it has to do with the way the two sides of our brains operate. It is thought that the left hemisphere is the critical, analytical side. Its function is to process numbers, evaluate data, and keep things neat and tidy. The right hemisphere, by contrast, is the intuitive, creative side. Its function is to think imaginatively, handle abstractions, and form and decipher stories. Storytelling and story listening are definitely right-brain activities.

The mental picture I have is that when story-based information is directed toward our brains, it gets routed to the right side, whereas numbers, statistics, and logical arguments are directed to the left side of the brain. Upon arrival, bundles of information sent to the left side (numbers, statistics, and logical arguments) are scrutinized and critiqued careful and skeptically, because that's what the left brain does.

Story-based information, on the other hand, is subject to less cynical review because that's the way the right brain operates. It's as if stories bypass the harsher scrub-down and go straight into the system. And since most of our important decisions are made intuitively and then later justified analytically, stories can be very potent in moving us to action. When it comes to touching hearts and affecting behavior, a well-placed story is almost always more effective than numbers, statistics, and logical arguments.

Stories Connect Us on a Human Level

I have learned that stories are the real ties that bind, regardless of the type of relationship. Sharing stories is an honoring, intimate experience that results in feelings of closeness and affection.

Sharing stories is the best way in the world to connect with people, to understand them, and for them to feel understood. We create genuine human connection by sharing the stories of our lives. As we share experiences back and forth, we start connecting on a personal level. It's very natural and comfortable.

I believe that we human beings are hardwired to connect with each other through story and to share important information, both factual and emotional, by sharing stories. For thousands of years, we sat around the community fire sharing the events of the day. We sat on the porch and rocked and talked about life. We shared happenings at the family table. We told our children stories at bedtime. We hung around the fishing hole weaving tales waiting for the fish to bite.

Today, however, with televisions and iPods, text messaging and life's busy pace, we don't seem to have nearly as much time for story sharing. Nevertheless, I think it is still a basic human need to tell stories and to hear them.

Stories Build Trust

Because this deep need to share stories is still strong within us but is so seldom honored in today's world, when you offer to listen and share stories with prospects and customers, they appreciate it and they connect with you. As a result, they start to feel comfortable with you and trust you. One of the most important things you can do in an initial meeting is to use stories to nurture a relationship of sufficient trust so that when you ultimately offer your advice, prospective customers will accept your recommendations and implement them.

The connective power of story is real and powerful regardless of whether the people involved have known each other for decades or have never met. I've seen how old friends can meet after years of absence, and with the telling of only a few tales of what they've each been doing in all that time, it's as if they were never apart. Stories re-ignite connections long dormant.

For people who have never met, stories can also fire up new relationships almost immediately. For many years I have taught a unique two-day professional training program called the Legacy Builder Retreat. On dozens of occasions, this Retreat has brought together a roomful of total strangers (in many cases hardened analytics like attorneys, financial planners, funeral directors, and accountants) in a sterile hotel meeting room, mixed them together randomly, and thrown them headlong into story-sharing activities.

The result: at the end of one day, complete strangers have become great friends. At the end of two days, the whole group is making plans to stay in touch, exchanging addresses and phone numbers, and promising to keep each other informed about matters in their professional and personal lives.

Stories Create Empathy and Understanding

By sharing stories, we are briefly able to see the world—or at least a part of it—from another's vantage point. We take in their words, their tone, and their body language through our senses and send them on to our minds, where they become the catalyst for our own internal reconstruction of the life experiences they are sharing with us. Their stories remake the neuron structure of our brains, and thus they literally become a part of us. True empathy and connection occur.

Just as story sharing builds human to human connections, conversely, whenever people reduce or terminate story sharing between themselves, their relationships are weakened. If you look closely at any relationship that is fading or already dead, you will find the parties to the relationship—whether friends, a married couple, family members, management and labor, or even nations—no longer share stories.

In fact, if you work back upstream to the point in time when the relationship turned from good to bad, you will discover it was at that moment that the parties stopped listening to each other's stories and stopped trying to tell them to each other. I'm not sure which is cause and which is effect, but I'm certain that, left unchecked, the cessation of story sharing is an unmistakable harbinger of the death of the relationship. Strong and lasting human relationships require the sharing of stories.

A Secret about Stories

We connect with those who listen to our stories, and we cherish those whose stories we have truly heard. Through stories, we understand their world and they understand ours.

The fact that this can happen quickly, almost immediately, is one of the keys to the Double Your Sales process. When two people meet at the story level, they don't need decades of memories to create a meaningful friendship. They become friends by creating a positive story of their future together. Friendships turn prospects into customers.

The Double Your Sales Professional Selling Process is based on these principles. It uses story to connect, to humanize, to warn, to encourage, to clarify, and to share information, both personal and professional. Most importantly, it uses stories to create between you and prospective customers a shared narrative of your future together. It allows both you and them to visualize a tomorrow in which you are working together for your mutual benefit. Without that, few if any sales are likely to happen.

Fortunately, you don't have to become a professional storyteller to be a successful salesperson. You don't have to understand all the details about stories and how they work, any more than you must be able to service a modern computerized, fuel-injected automobile to successfully drive it. It doesn't hurt to know those things, but it's definitely not required. Your innate skills as a storyteller and a story listener, with a little practice and a little polish and with the story sequence built into the process, will be enough.

Once you understand the rationale behind the Double Your Sales process, you'll see that the stories within it are simple and natural and thus easy to learn and apply. The next chapter will help you appreciate the "intuitive logic" behind this process.

Why the Double Your Sales Process Isn't "StorySelling"

Because The Double Your Sales Professional Selling Process is about selling and because of its extensive use of stories, it's not surprising that some who have a superficial understanding of it confuse it with another methodology called "StorySelling." That term was coined in 2000 by

Scott West and Mitch Anthony in *StorySelling for Financial Advisors.*
That was an insightful book and I applaud its central message. In it the
authors wrote:

> The way top advisors sell is by simplifying matters, not
> complicating them. Many advisors purposefully add complexi-
> ty to their presentations, thinking it raises their stature and
> indispensability in the eyes of their clients. This complicated
> approach, however, works against, not for, the advisor

> The top producers we found did just the opposite with
> amazing results. By using simple illustrations, anecdotes, and
> metaphors, they bring themselves and their ideas into the men-
> tal grasp of every client. Consequently, clients love talking to
> them and referring their friends as well.

> We call this selling technique storyselling. We have come to
> believe that storyselling is the key to building a large and loyal
> book of business. It is a proven psychological fact that story-
> telling puts the mind in a light trancelike state and makes us
> more susceptible to influence. Everyone loves a good story.

When it first appeared, the West/Anthony approach was light years
ahead of the other sales techniques of its time. Since then, the term
"StorySelling" and the methodology the book presented have sprouted
legs and taken on a life of their own. Now, it seems, "StorySelling" has
become a burgeoning family of sales techniques, each a little different
from the others but all united by the way stories are used during the
sales meeting.

The approach set forth in this book, the Double Your Sales process,
does not belong to the StorySelling family. The way this approach uses
stories is very different from the original West/Anthony StorySelling
technique and all its progeny.

In some StorySelling approaches, stories are like magic grenades. They are carefully guarded until, at the ideal moment in the exchange, the salesperson reaches into his satchel of stories, grabs just the right one for the issue or prospect in question, and lobs it artfully in the prospect's direction. The goal is to "put the [prospect's] mind in a light trancelike state" and make them more "susceptible to [the salesperson's] influence."

In other StorySelling approaches, stories are like silver bullets, almost mystical in their defensive impact. When the prospect raises a tough objection or offers stiff resistance, the salesperson can fire off a certain story, like a round from a revolver, and drop the objection or resistance in its tracks.

By contrast, in the Double Your Sales process, stories are not something you do *to* your prospects, they are something you share and create *with* your prospects. In this approach, stories are part of a graceful and elegant interaction. This approach is a dance, not a march; it's a conversation, not a sparring match.

Of course you tell stories in the Double Your Sales process, but the most important stories are the ones you help your prospects imagine and share with you. In response to your attentive listening and your thoughtful story-leading questions, their stories drive the process as much or even more than your stories.

Chapter Summary

- The best way to communicate with prospective clients is through stories.

- Stories are our native language. As a result, when you speak in the language of story, people can grasp more of what you say and they will feel more at ease.

- Stories allow our brains to receive, process, retain, and recall far more information than they otherwise could handle.

- We are defined more by the stories we have formed about the experiences of our lives than by the experiences themselves.

- Story-based information is more readily received and believed by our brains than other forms of input.

- Sharing stories is the best way to empathize with people, to understand them, and help them feel understood. We create genuine human connection by sharing the stories of our lives.

- The Double Your Sales process uses story to connect, to humanize, to warn, to encourage, to clarify, and to share information. Most importantly, it uses stories to create between you and prospective customers a shared narrative of your future together. It allows both you and them to visualize a tomorrow in which you are working together for your mutual benefit.

- A basic understanding of how stories work helps you master the Double Your Sales process more readily, but because sharing stories is already built into the way our brains operate, a deep or involved study of the subject is not required.

- The Double Your Sales approach is not part of the "StorySelling" genre of sales techniques. The Double Your Sales process is based on the interactive creation and exchange of stories between prospective customers and the salesperson, not simply on the salesperson lobbing "magical" stories at the prospect.

- In the Double Your Sales approach, stories are not something you do *to* your prospects, they are something you share and create *with* your prospects. In this approach, stories are part of a graceful interaction, not a verbal sparing match.

Chapter 4

Mr. Analytical and Mr. Intuitive

Key Points

➤ When it comes to selling, the side of the prospective customers' brain that is in the dominant role at any given moment of the sales meeting will determine what type of information you should offer and whether they are likely to buy.

➤ You must learn to recognize when you are speaking to Mr. Analytical or to Mr. Intuitive, and you must learn how to shift prospective customers from one side of their brain to the other.

➤ This ability is an art, not a science, and it will come to you quickly and naturally as you start to use the Double Your Sales process.

Brain Structure

We have two hemispheres or sides to our brains. The two hemispheres take significantly different approaches to guiding our actions, processing information, understanding the world, and reacting to events. Both sides work together and both are at work all the time, but each side carries out different functions. These different functions address different questions and issues.

It is vitally important to understand that in sales meetings with prospective customers, the side of their brains that is dominating their thinking at any given moment is a huge issue. It is largely determinative of their ability to receive the information you are trying to share with them and the likelihood they will answer "yes" when it comes time to make a buying decision.

Mr. Analytical

In *A Whole New Mind,* Daniel Pink explains that the left hemisphere is sequential, focuses on text, and analyzes details. The left brain specializes in analysis, and thus in my teaching I often refer to the left side as "Mr. Analytical."

Mr. Analytical loves numbers. It's like there's a little calculator running all the time in there, crunching number after number. Mr. Analytical also likes things to be literal and concrete. He doesn't care so much for abstractions.

Mr. Analytical figures things out by breaking them down, component by component. He's like the kid who figures out how the watch works by taking it apart, piece by piece.

Mr. Analytical never seems to get enough information. He wants more, more, more—more data, more numbers, more statistics—but he never seems to be able to get enough. And why is that? No less a mind than Albert Einstein thought about that question, and he came upon a brilliant way to explain what is happening.

Einstein suggested that you could graph everything a person knows as a circle. The area inside the circle represents all the information known to that person. The perimeter or circumference of the circle, he said, thus represents the interface of everything that person doesn't know.

If you increase the amount of information the person knows, thus making the area of the circle larger, what happens to the circumference? It too becomes larger. Thus, the more the person knows, the more they realize they don't know. This realization causes them to crave even more information. Alas, when they feed that craving, the cycle is repeated: the more information they get, the more they realize they don't know, the more uncertainty they experience, and the more additional information they want.

Mr. Analytical demands greater certainty, but given the nature of the world and the nature of information, he can't get it. The net result is that, at decision-making time, Mr. Analytical locks up. He goes into "analysis paralysis." He is unable to go forward.

If you're trying to sell to Mr. Analytical, it can get ugly. For him, the answer is usually "no," or at least "not now." At best, he wants to go home and think about it.

Some years ago I was teaching this material at a workshop in Phoenix. After describing Mr. Analytical to the class, I asked if anyone had ever met him. Of course everyone laughed, because once I had described him, they all knew they'd seen him lots of times and had tried to sell to him.

One woman volunteered that not only had she met him, she was married to him. I asked her to tell us more. She said her husband was a CPA who was totally absorbed with numbers. He responded to situations just like the Mr. Analytical I had described. Pushing her a bit further, I asked her to give us an example of her husband's "Mr. Analytical" patterns.

"Well, clearly the most extreme example," she said, "was our honeymoon."

"What do you mean?" I queried, just a little nervous about where this was going.

"Let's just say he planned the whole honeymoon using an Excel spreadsheet," she answered. The whole class fell apart in laughter.

Here's a summary of what Mr. Analytical looks like in a sales situation:

Mr. Analytical

— Responds to numbers

— Needs concrete examples

— Breaks things into pieces

— Never gets enough information

— More information = more procrastination

— Demands detailed certainty

— Analysis paralysis

Mr. Intuitive

Everyone, even the most serious CPAs, brain surgeons, and engineers, also has a right side of their brain. In discussing the right hemisphere, Daniel Pink explains that the right hemisphere is simultaneous rather than sequential, specializes in context rather than in text, and synthesizes the big picture rather than analyzes the details.

When I teach, I often refer to the right side of the brain as "Mr. Intuitive." Mr. Intuitive loves visual and graphic images. He is able to see the big picture. Mr. Intuitive can project into the future. He can imagine how the present moment can extend ahead in time.

He understands things by putting them together. He likes to see how different things connect. When he finds gaps, he's not stymied or stuck. He can extrapolate from what is known and fill in what is missing or unknown.

Because he is aware of how things feel, Mr. Intuitive is comfortable going with his gut. He is able to put things together, take a leap of faith, make a decision, and move forward.

Here's a summary of what Mr. Intuitive looks like in a sales situation:

Mr. Intuitive

— Responds to images

— Can imagine the future

— Puts it all together

— Fills in the gaps

— Gets a gut feeling

— Takes a leap of faith

— Decides and moves forward

When It Comes to Selling, Side Matters

For the sake of literal accuracy, let me repeat what I said above. Both sides of the brain work together and both sides are at work all the time. One hemisphere does not switch off when the other switches on.

But at different moments in a sales meeting (and in most other contexts), one side or the other of the prospective customers' brains is usually in the dominant or lead role. The side of the prospective customers' brain that is dominating their thinking at any given moment determines whether they can receive certain types of information and determines the likelihood that they will say "yes" to an invitation to buy.

Many years of observation and experience have convinced me that virtually every major decision a person makes is an intuitive, right-brain decision first that is subsequently justified or buttressed analytically.

You can see this phenomenon if you examine the major decisions in your own life, such as where to go to school, what to study, what job to take, where to live, whether to marry, who to marry, what house to buy, whether to have children, etc. In nearly every case, you made the decision with your gut and then you looked for reasons to show that your decision made sense.

Because of this fact, it is critical to understand that "side matters" when it comes to selling. The decision to make a major purchase is a big deal for most prospective customers. Consequently, I believe every person you have ever sold to was predominantly Mr. Intuitive—in their right mind—at the moment of sale. The intuitive side was the one that decided to make the purchase.

But then Mr. Analytical got involved, seeking to rationalize the decision. If Mr. Analytical couldn't adequately justify the buying decision, or if he felt slighted in the process, he may have fought back and you may have lost the sale.

Prospective customers will shift from one side of the brain to the other many times during the course of a sales meeting. If you are unaware of those shifts, or if you are unable to influence those shifts, you'll get blind-sided during the meeting and you may get clobbered later on when Mr. Analytical causes "buyer's remorse."

Five Keys to Working with Mr. Analytical and Mr. Intuitive

There are five keys to working with Mr. Analytical and Mr. Intuitive in a sales meeting setting.

1] You must learn to recognize whether Mr. Analytical or Mr. Intuitive is dominant with prospective customers at any given moment in the sales meeting.

2] Once you recognize whether Mr. Analytical or Mr. Intuitive is dominant, you must be able to meet prospective customers where they are—either in their right or left mind.

3] You must be able to shift prospective customers from one side of the brain to the other at different points in the sales meeting.

4] You shift prospective customers back and forth between Mr. Analytical and Mr. Intuitive by asking certain types of questions or offering certain types of information.

5] Visualization and story sharing are predominantly right-brain activities. Analysis, calculation, logic, and ordering are predominantly left-brain activities. Thus, asking visualization or story-leading questions or offering visual or story-based information will invite Mr. Intuitive to the fore. On the other hand, asking questions calling for analysis, calculations, logic, or ranking, or offering number-based information will invite Mr. Analytical to take the lead.

The ability to utilize this left brain/right brain phenomenon in a sales meeting is an art, not a science. Over time, as you pay attention to the Mr. Analytical/Mr. Intuitive issue, and as you learn to use the Double Your Sales process, you will become increasingly more graceful and more effective at using it. In the meantime, here are some guidelines to help you get started.

1] Nearly all prospective customers will begin a sales meeting on the analytical side of their brain. This is natural and normal. Mr. Analytical is more guarded and suspicious; he worries that just being there in front of a salesperson is dangerous. His defenses are up. To move forward effectively in the meeting, you must meet prospective customers on the left side of their brain.

2] Most of the sales meeting needs to be conducted on the intuitive or right side of the brain. It is much easier to introduce new information to prospective customers from the right side. It is also much easier to connect with them there.

3] Ultimately, when it is time for prospective customers to make a buying decision, they need to be in intuitive mode. Otherwise, your chances for a sale are slim.

4] Before the meeting is finished, you must intentionally turn the conversation analytical, so the decision to buy does not unravel, leaving you to wrestle with the dreaded "buyer's remorse."

Don't be too concerned that this may not be crystal clear to you yet. Once you start to learn the twelve stories that constitute the Double

Your Sales process, I will show you how the sequence itself is designed to keep prospective customers on the appropriate side of their brains all the way through the sales meeting. In almost no time, this Mr. Analytical/Mr. Intuitive approach will become second nature to you. When that happens, you'll be well on your way to doubling your sales.

Chapter Summary

- The two sides of our brain work together and both are at work all the time, but they carry out different functions and address different questions and issues.

- The left side of the brain—what I call "Mr. Analytical"—likes numbers and an endless supply of information. Unfortunately, his need for endless information and certainty usually cannot be satisfied, so he often locks up in "analysis paralysis."

- The right side of the brain—what I call "Mr. Intuitive"—likes images and visualizing the future. He can put the big picture together and fill in the gaps. Mr. Intuitive can act on gut feelings, make a decision, and move forward.

- Whichever side of the brain is in the dominant role at any given moment during a sales meeting will determine what type of information can be received and the likelihood that prospective customers will decide to buy.

- Virtually every major decision we make is first made intuitively and then justified analytically. Buying from you is a major decision for most of your prospective customers.

- To double your sales you must be able to:

  — Recognize which side of the brain is dominant at any given moment with prospective customers.
  — Meet prospective customers where they are.
  — Use certain types of questions or information to shift prospective customers from one side of the brain to the other.

- Asking visualization or story-leading questions or offering visual or story-based information will invite Mr. Intuitive to the fore; whereas asking questions calling for analysis, calculations, logic, or ordering, or offering number-based information will invite Mr. Analytical to take the lead.

- Understanding and using this Mr. Analytical/Mr. Intuitive approach is an art, not a science. You skill in using it elegantly and effectively will develop quickly as you use the Double Your Sales process.

Chapter 5

The Whole and
The Sum of the Parts

Key Points

➤ This process works best as an intact whole, but many of its parts have great stand-alone value in other selling processes and in other applications.

➤ This process is intended to be only one part of a company's business development system. If other parts of that system are weak, you may need to invest in other programs.

➤ Our specialty is helping you close more business when you sit down face to face with prospects and potential repeat customers.

Use It Whole or Use the Parts

The Double Your Sales approach presented in this book is a unified process for turning prospects into customers. It is most powerful when used as a complete, intact process. Used from start to finish in sequence, it is virtually guaranteed to improve your sales results. It has its own "intuitive logic," its own rationale for how and why it works.

In addition, you may find that certain pieces of it have great stand-alone value for you, either as part of an existing selling process that works in your unique situation, or in other applications, such as speeches or presentations. Feel free to take what fits and make it work for you.

I compare this aspect of this process to my favorite music group of all time, the Beatles. As a unit, the Fab Four created some of the most moving and innovative music of the 20th Century. They seemed to drive each other on and push each other forward, so that the band was always on the cutting edge.

It was a sad day for me when Paul announced they were disbanding the group. But that didn't mark the end of their music; it just marked the end of their music together. All four enjoyed wildly successful solo careers, including Ringo who was thought to be the least talented musician of the bunch. From their break-up, we were able to see the depth of the talent pool the four of them had been drawing upon as the Beatles.

The same is true of the twelve pieces that make up the Double Your Sales process. There's an unrivaled synergy when the whole group is working together as a unified system. But at the same time, some of the pieces are superstars in their own right. To me, The New Me Story, The Hidden Waterfall Story, The Consequences Story, and The Dress Rehearsal Story could easily qualify as the John, Paul, George, and Ringo of the Double Your Sales ensemble. And I could have just as easily named several others to that list. (It's not easy to pick favorites when all of them are your "children.")

So go ahead and use these components as you see fit, either as a whole or as part of your own selling process, in speeches, or other places. They'll serve you well.

This Isn't a Marketing, Prospect Management, or Sales Management System

There are wonderful programs out there for helping you present your message to the marketplace and generate qualified leads. There are wonderful programs out there to help you track and follow up on all your prospects. There are wonderful programs out there that can help sales managers support and encourage their salespeople. There are even programs out there that claim to be able to help you do all of the above.

This process doesn't do any of that.

This process will help you close more business when you sit down face to face with prospects and customers. That's all it does, but it does that remarkably well. Don't frustrate yourself by trying to make this process do or be something it wasn't built for.

Obviously, if you aren't getting in front of enough prospects, or you are losing track of your prospects, or your sales staff is disorganized and undisciplined, you may need to invest in other programs or system to handle those aspects of your business development agenda. Without those things in place, even the best selling process in the world cannot, by itself, deliver what you need.

But, if the weak link in your supply chain for delivering more customers to your business is in the sales meeting itself, you've come to the right place. Get ready now, because you're about to learn how to DOUBLE YOUR SALES.

Chapter Summary

- The Double Your Sales process is most effective as a synchronistic unit, used as a whole and in sequence.

- The different components of the process can also be used effectively as stand-alone tools and stories in a variety of settings.

- The Double Your Sales process is designed to help you close more business in a face-to-face setting with prospective customers. It is not designed as a marketing program, as a system to manage prospects and contacts, or as an approach to sales management.

- Used properly and for the appropriate purpose, this approach will Double Your Sales.

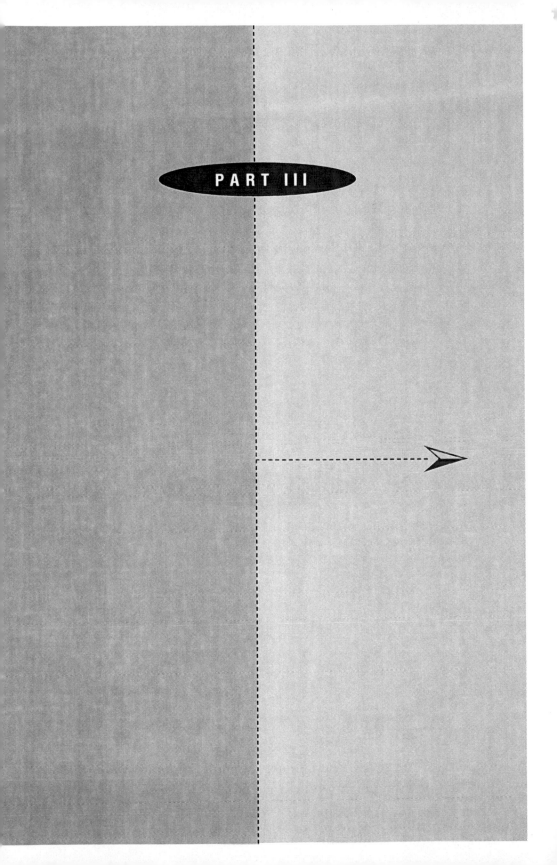

PART III

Chapter 6

The Banana/Lettuce Story

Key Points

> Managing the expectations of prospective customers is one key to a successful sales meeting.

> Prospective customers usually come to a sales meeting in analytical mode. You need to meet them there and then gently move them to intuitive mode.

> When you tell The Banana/Lettuce Story, you outline what you expect to accomplish in the meeting; you inquire as to what prospective customers need and want from the meeting; and then you create and describe aloud a consensus agenda based on both sets of expectations.

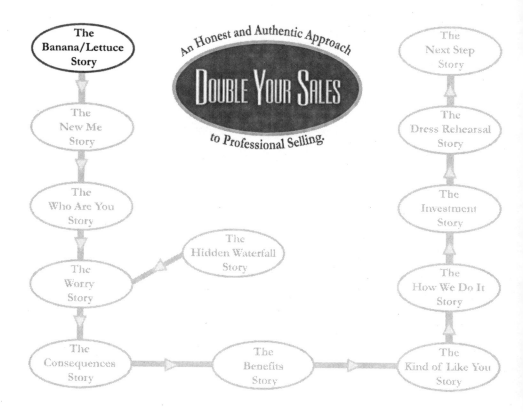

The Banana/Lettuce Story

An Honest and Authentic Approach

DOUBLE YOUR SALES

to Professional Selling.

The New Me Story

The Who Are You Story

The Worry Story

The Hidden Waterfall Story

The Consequences Story

The Benefits Story

The Kind of Like You Story

The How We Do It Story

The Investment Story

The Dress Rehearsal Story

The Next Step Story

What is The Banana/Lettuce Story?

If I were to ask you to guess what a chimpanzee's favorite food is, you would probably guess, bananas. If you did, you would be correct. If I were to ask you to guess what a chimpanzee's second favorite food is, you probably wouldn't have a clue. You would probably guess some other kind of fruit, or nuts, or perhaps something sweet. The correct answer, as you have probably surmised from the title of this chapter, is lettuce. Believe it or not, chimpanzees like lettuce almost as much as bananas. Given a choice, a chimpanzee will pick lettuce nearly as often as bananas.

I have been asking that question about a chimpanzee's second favorite food for a number of years and never got a correct answer until a couple of years ago. I posed the question in a workshop in Denver and one of the participants raised his hand and said confidently, "I know, it's lettuce."

I asked him how he knew, because no one ever knows the right answer.

"Oh that's easy," he said. "I used to raise chimpanzees, and you're right. Chimps love lettuce almost as much as bananas."

A group of zoologists, aware that chimpanzees like bananas and lettuce almost equally, once conducted an interesting experiment. Using two similar groups of chimps, they placed one group in a closed room with a door leading out to a cage. In the cage, they placed a wooden box and under the wooden box, they placed heads of lettuce. They opened the door to the room and allowed the chimpanzees into the cage. The chimpanzees discovered the box, lifted it up, and found lettuce, their second favorite food. As you might imagine, they were delighted to find the lettuce and began to eat it excitedly.

The second group of chimpanzees was placed in a similar environment, with one exception. Between the room and the cage, there was a window with open curtains through which the chimps could see into the cage. The zoologists, in plain sight of the chimpanzees, placed a bunch of bananas under the wooden box. Then they closed the curtains, removed the bananas, and replaced them with heads of lettuce. They opened the door to the room and the chimpanzees were allowed into the cage. They went straight for the box, lifted it up, and discovered lettuce, their second favorite food. How do you suppose they responded?

Rather than being happy to find their second favorite food, these chimpanzees, unlike the first group, went absolutely berserk! They shrieked in anger, shredded the lettuce, and stamped on it. They went totally "ape."

Remember, these chimpanzees hadn't discovered under the box something they hated; they had found lettuce, their second favorite food. But instead of eating it contentedly like the first group, they went ballistic. What was the difference?

Obviously, the difference was their expectations. The first group had no expectation of finding bananas under the box, and thus they were quite happy when they discovered lettuce there. The second group, however, expected to find bananas. When they found lettuce instead, their expectations were thwarted.

To the degree that we can extrapolate from chimp behavior to human behavior, there is a significant lesson here. When people's expectations aren't met, even when they are offered something they would otherwise cherish, they will often become irrational and even angry.

This principle is especially true in a sales setting. My own experience has taught me that one of the keys to a successful sales meeting is to manage prospective customers' expectations.

The Banana/Lettuce Story is the name we give to the opening narrative in a Double Your Sales meeting with prospective customers. We **do not** tell prospective customers about the experiment with chimps, bananas, and lettuce. Instead, we make sure their expectations as to what the meeting will look like are aligned with ours. We use "The Banana/Lettuce Story" nomenclature in teaching the Double Your Sales process in order to remind students of the serious consequences of not managing the expectations of prospective customers.

When you tell The Banana/Lettuce Story in an actual meeting with prospective customers, you should outline what you expect to accomplish in the meeting; inquire as to what they need and want from the meeting; and then create and describe aloud a consensus agenda based on both sets of expectations.

What is the Purpose of The Banana/Lettuce Story?

The purpose of The Banana/Lettuce Story is to make sure prospective customers' expectations are understood and are in harmony with yours, so that the meeting lives up to those expectations. Based on the chimpanzee experiment described earlier and on my own experience, I have learned that if prospective customers' expectations are not met, even though what I am offering may be wonderful and something they would otherwise appreciate, the meeting is bound to fail.

Thus The Banana/Lettuce Story makes sure they know what to expect, you know what to expect, and everyone ends up having a satisfactory experience. If The Banana/Lettuce Story is not handled correctly, it can nullify everything else in the meeting. If it is used correctly, the 11 other stories in the Double Your Sales model will be much more powerful and much more likely to lead to a sale.

What is an Example of The Banana/Lettuce Story?

Here is what The Banana/Lettuce Story might sound like with prospective customers. After greeting them warmly, engaging in cordial conversation, and making sure they are comfortable, you would say something like the following.

I've been looking forward to our meeting this morning. I'm glad that both of you are able to be here. I've set aside about an hour for our visit. Is that about how much time you were expecting?

Let me outline for you my thoughts about how this meeting might proceed, and then I'd like to hear your ideas as well.

Once we get started, I'd first like to tell you a little bit about myself and the way my practice is different from other advisors with whom you may have worked in the past. Then I'd like to learn about you so I can understand a bit more about your backgrounds. Then I want to dig in immediately and talk about the concerns you have that brought you to my office today. After we identify some of those concerns, I want to get your perspective on what it would mean to you if those concerns were not properly addressed, and then on the other hand, what it would mean to you if we could find solutions to those concerns.

Once I know what your concerns are, I can describe some other cases I've worked on that were similar to yours. I can also tell you about the process we would use to work together to create great solutions for your particular situation.

I'm sure you have questions about what it costs for our services, and I want to be very transparent about that. Once I understand your concerns and what possible services we might be called upon to render for you, and I've had a chance to share with you the process we will use if we work together, I will talk candidly and openly about what your investment would be if we decide to work together.

Of course I want to make sure that all of your questions are answered and that you leave here with a clear picture of what it would look like for us to work together, so we'll save time to review everything we've covered and to decide what the next step will be. Does that sound like what you were expecting this meeting to be?

What else would you like to include in our agenda?

It sounds like we're all on the same page, so let's get started.

How Do You Use The Banana/Lettuce Story?

You use this story to set the tone for the rest of the sales meeting. The Banana/Lettuce Story provides the footing for the bridge from the analytical side of the brain to the intuitive side of the brain.

Prospective customers will come into a sales meeting with their guard up. They will be in analytical mode and thus they will be analyzing, evaluating, critiquing, and perhaps criticizing whatever they encounter. It's important to first meet people where they are and then invite them to a different place. Accordingly, you need to meet prospective customers in analytical mode.

For this reason, you should begin The Banana/Lettuce Story analytically by discussing the length of the meeting, the sequential details of the meeting, and other mechanical aspects of the meeting. This will engage the left side of prospective customers' brains and help Mr. Analytical feel relevant and comfortable in the meeting.

Once there, you should start easing them toward the intuitive mode, which is where all buying decisions are initially made. You do that by moving into a narrative of your expected flow of the meeting. Allow your prospective customers to picture the meeting in their own minds, based on your narrative. Then invite them to suggest adjustments to the narrative according to their needs and expectations. Discuss how your ideas and their ideas can be meshed to create a collaborative agenda, so that everyone is in agreement about what the meeting will look like. When you have achieved consensus, summarize in narrative fashion what you have agreed to.

Sales meetings that begin with an effective Banana/Lettuce Story flow smoothly and comfortably. Agreeing on the agenda for the meeting creates a sense of ease among all present. Inviting prospective customers to accept or adjust the agenda as proposed helps them feel a sense of ownership for the meeting as well.

What Are Some Tips For Using The Banana/Lettuce Story?

I recently conducted a sales meeting that included three couples, their two in-house CPAs, another professional advisor, and me. The meeting was intended to last nearly four hours. In situations like that, with such a long meeting and so many parties involved, the odds were high that expectations would be so diverse that the meeting would ultimately run off the track and crash into chaos.

However, by using the 12-step Double Your Sales model as my proposed agenda, I was able to outline the flow of the meeting in a way that was clear and understandable to all. The prospective customers were able to suggest changes they wanted based on time schedules and other concerns and expectations. The ten people in the room then came easily to a united consensus as to the tone, time, and flow of the meeting.

The result was a powerful and effective sales meeting experience. During those four hours, my purposes were accomplished and the prospective customers' issues and concerns were comfortably addressed. This created an ideal setting for them to make a decision to retain my company and use our services.

One of the keys to delivering The Banana/Lettuce Story successfully is to have a clear sense in your own mind of what the meeting needs to look like. If you don't know what you want the meeting to be like, how can you describe it in narrative fashion to prospective customers? It is essential that you be perfectly clear and comfortable with your meeting format, so that you can have a base from which to build an agreed-upon meeting agenda with prospective customers.

Another key is to make sure that you present the proposed agenda in a manner and with a tone that authentically invites prospective customers to tell you additions or modifications they would like to make. Unless they genuinely sense that the creation of the agenda is a joint project, it is quite likely that prospective customers will hold back and not share their real concerns, which will result in the meeting going forward without true consensus. Thus, projecting an inviting and open spirit of cooperation is essential for a successful Banana/Lettuce Story.

Some people use a printed agenda for their engagement meetings, and some even send the agenda to prospective customers prior to the beginning of the meeting. I personally prefer to discuss the agenda orally, so I do not present a written agenda. In my view, a written agenda makes the meeting too formal and too analytical, making it harder for prospective customers to feel they can have any real input in the design of the agenda. To them, it may feel a lot like "take it or leave it."

Without a quality Banana/Lettuce Story to anchor the meeting, your intentions may be misunderstood, the prospective customers' needs may not be clear and articulated, and the two sides' expectations may not be effectively meshed before the meeting proceeds. As a result, without upfront consensus, prospective customers may raise certain issues (such as price) at times that are inconsistent with your vision of the meeting. When that happens, even a small misunderstanding can cause the sales meeting to fizzle out, or even crash and burn. If that occurs, not only is the sales meeting itself wasted, but the relationship with those prospective customers may be permanently damaged.

One of the most critical concerns prospective customers bring to a sales meeting is the question of price. I believe it is important that cost figures be presented to prospective customers only when they have sufficient information about the value of your services or products to be able to make sense of the numbers. If given too early, cost figures are misleading or meaningless.

For example, if I were to offer to sell you a used car for $5,000, how would you respond? Would that be a fair price or not? Obviously, if the used car in question were a 20-year-old rusted-out clunker, $5,000 would be way too much money. On the other hand, if the used car in question were a year-old Mercedes convertible in prime condition, $5,000 would be an outrageously good deal. So whether $5,000 for a used car is a good deal or not depends entirely upon the context.

In the same way, whether your prices are too high, too low, or just right cannot be appropriately determined unless prospective customers have an accurate sense of the value you will be providing. As a result, often you will need to delay a discussion of price until you have provided them sufficient background and understanding to compare price to value.

Unfortunately, prospective customers may feel anxious or nervous if they are left during the bulk of the sales meeting not knowing what you might charge them. They may even feel that your refusal to talk about price early in the meeting indicates that you are playing games with them or being disingenuous.

The solution to this dilemma is to address their price concerns as early as possible, not by telling them what the price will be (unless it can be done in a way that allows them to understand the context), but rather by stating specifically WHEN you will cover it and WHY it is appropriate to wait to do so, explaining that they need to have a context for understanding the number. You must make it clear that you are not trying to be hide the ball or avoid an honest discussion of the value and cost of your services.

I've learned that it helps to strike preemptively with this part of the Banana/Lettuce Story, because if they ask me first about price, then it's much more difficult to not sound defensive or evasive in my response. On the other hand, if I bring it up first by pointing out the place in the agenda where we will discuss price, and if I explain my reasons for waiting until that time, it's much easier to make them feel comfortable with the price issue.

How Do You Create The Banana/Lettuce Story?

If you use the Double Your Sales process as the pattern for your sales meetings, creating your own Banana/Lettuce Story is quite easy. You can use the sample story given above pretty much as is. If you follow your own process for your sales meetings, you will need to modify the example given above, based on how you vary from the Double Your Sales model.

In either case, to create your own Banana/Lettuce Story, you should first discuss mechanical issues such as the length of the meeting, and then describe the steps of your meeting in narrative fashion. It's important to explain each step in a way that makes sense from the prospective customers' point of view. In other words, instead of saying "I'm going to tell my New Me Story," you should say, "I'm going to tell you a little bit about me and my philosophy of practice," or something like that.

Instead of saying, "Then I'd like you to tell me the Who Are You? Story," you should say instead, "Then I'd like to hear something about you and where you came from and what brings you here today." That's what I mean, when I say you should explain each step of your process from the point of view of prospective customers.

After you have laid out your ideas of what the meeting ought to look like, you need to open the discussion to the customers' expectations of the meeting. Once you understand what they are expecting, you need to create a joint agenda in which everyone's expectations are fairly and appropriately addressed. You then need to re-narrate the consensus agenda to confirm that everyone is on board with it. When everyone's expectations are in alignment, you're ready to move on to The New Me Story.

How Do You Get Started Using The Banana/Lettuce Story?

In order to get started using The Banana/Lettuce Story, you need to first get clear about your agenda for your sales meetings. Then I recommend you practice describing your preferred agenda to a colleague, friend, or family member using language and descriptions that are friendly to the prospective customers' point of view. I believe that role-playing in this situation is important and very useful. Once you feel comfortable telling the story in a role-playing situation, you should start trying it with real people in real sales situations. Perfection is not required; close enough is good enough in this environment.

Chapter Summary

- Human beings, like chimpanzees, will sometimes reject something they like simply because it does not meet their expectations. Managing expectations is absolutely essential to a successful sales meeting.

- Prospective customers will come to a sales meeting in an analytical mode. We must meet them where they are by focusing first on the length and other "mechanical" aspects of the meeting. Then we need to invite them to move to the intuitive mode.

- Moving to the intuitive mode is done most effectively by narrating how you expect the meeting to go and then inviting them to help you refine the narrative so that it addresses their expectations of the meeting.

- Once you have shared your expectations and the prospective customers have shared theirs, you need to construct a joint agenda that meshes the needs and expectations of everyone in the meeting.

- It is essential that prospective customers' expectations concerning the discussion of price are addressed early in the conversation and in a way that assures them that you are not dodging the issue or playing games with them.

- Once everyone is comfortable with the proposed agenda, and everyone's expectations of the meeting are in alignment, you are ready to move on to The New Me Story.

- Role playing and practice are important in helping you prepare to present the Banana/Lettuce story in a real sales meeting.

Chapter 7

The New Me Story

Key Points

➤ The New Me Story humanizes and personalizes you, and makes you more credible and approachable.

➤ The New Me Story is a key step in shifting the sales meeting to the right, intuitive side of the brain where buying decisions are initially made.

➤ The New Me Story utilizes the traditional story arc and follows a simple pattern:

- *Step one: "the old me."* This is who you used to be.
- *Step two: "the transforming event."* Something happened that rattled your world.
- *Step three: "the response."* You initially reacted badly, but then your better self took over and you changed, becoming a much better, more qualified, competent person.
- *Step four: "the new me."* As a result of your response to the transforming event, you are now more capable of helping prospective customers solve their problems.

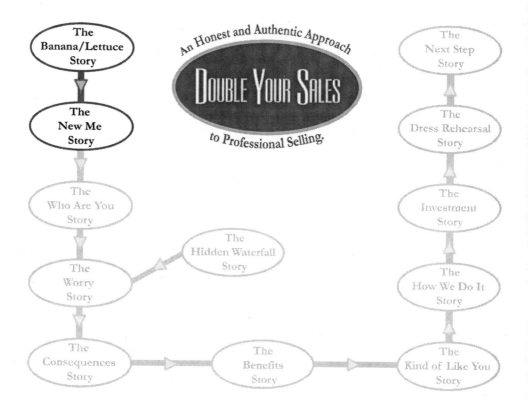

The Banana/Lettuce Story

The New Me Story

An Honest and Authentic Approach

DOUBLE YOUR SALES

to Professional Selling.

The Next Step Story

The Dress Rehearsal Story

The Who Are You Story

The Investment Story

The Hidden Waterfall Story

The Worry Story

The How We Do It Story

The Consequences Story

The Benefits Story

The Kind of Like You Story

What is The New Me Story?

The New Me Story is a brief and effective way to introduce your-self to prospective customers and to shift the sales meeting to the right, intuitive side of the brain where buying decisions are made. The New Me Story helps prospective customers see you as a real person, someone who has experienced real life, and made change for the better, in the process becoming someone who is more capable of helping them address their concerns and find appropriate solutions to their problems.

The New Me Story utilizes the traditional story arc, which is found in all good literature, movies, and television programs. It paints a picture of who you used to be, identifies an event that shook up your world, describes your struggle to deal with that event, and celebrates your eventual improvement because of that event.

What is the Purpose of The New Me Story?

The New Me Story is a way of saying to the listener, "*I have experienced real life.*" One thing we know about real life is that it is about dealing with a constantly changing world. Real people have to grow and develop. Real people have to wrestle with external and internal forces that force them to respond to their environment.

The New Me Story shows that you are not plastic, you're not a façade, not just a face and a title like "estate planner" or "certified financial planner" or whatever your title might be. Instead, you're a real person living your life in a real and challenging world. The New Me Story helps the listener perceive you in more human terms. In other words, you become more real and approachable when you tell an interesting and effective New Me Story.

The New Me Story also serves to foster sharing and connection between the teller and the listener. Your words invite prospective customers to create their own mental images of the events being described. In their mind's eye, they see you and a little slice of your life. With a good story, they actually dedicate a small piece of their neuron structure to that episode of your history. You've now become a part of them. And because of that, they will feel more comfortable telling you their stories.

The New Me Story also gives prospective customers permission and encouragement to make their own changes. The New Me Story says in a subtle yet powerful way, "*I changed and so can you. Go ahead, make that leap from prospect to customer. It's okay.*" In this way, your story of change can be the catalyst, the spark that ignites their transformation.

Telling The New Me Story shifts the whole dynamic of a sales meeting. Most of the time, when meeting with someone who is trying to sell them something, prospective customers are guarded, skeptical, and concerned someone's going to take advantage of them. In some cases, they may feel intimidated. They're often in the left side of their brain because they know they're going to have to process some complicated information.

Prospective customers who are in the left side of the brain, in analytical or critical mode, are much less likely to move forward. Remember, virtually every major decision we've made in our lives— whether it was to buy this house or to move or to marry or to go to that college—was first decided on an intuitive level, on the right side of the brain, and then it was rationalized on the left side of the brain.

So, if you want prospective customers to move forward and make the transformation from prospect to customer, you need to address the right side of the brain. You do that best by shifting the conversation into story-sharing mode. You can make that shift happen by telling your New Me Story.

What Does The New Me Story Sound Like?

The following is a New Me Story I use in my work helping estate planners and financial advisors become Certified Legacy Advisors.

Here's an experience I had a few years ago. In the late 1980's, I was the head of the Trust Department for a community bank in Brookhaven, Mississippi, a small town of about 10,000 people located midway between New Orleans, Louisiana, and Jackson, Mississippi.

On April Fools Day 1989, I left the bank where I had worked for five years and set up my own office. All the other attorneys in town were convinced I was going to starve to death in a town as small as Brookhaven because I announced I wasn't going to do all that messy stuff they had to deal with like divorces, personal injury litigation, and criminal matters. Instead, I was going to focus on estate planning and asset management.

Fast forward a few years to 1996, and I had defied all their expectations. Things were going well with me. I had a thriving estate planning and asset management practice. I owned the business and I owned the building where I had my offices. I had four full-time employees. My accountant said as far as he knew, I was the best-paid attorney in town, including all the personal injury lawyers. Best of all for me, I was taking off 165 days a year. I felt like I had arrived. I was ready to coast to a serene and comfortable retirement.

One day I was going through some draft estate planning documents with a client and somewhere around page 27 or so, he stopped me and said, "*You know, Mr. Farnsworth, back when we were talking about this, we had a lot of conversations about family values, about the things that I really wanted for my children and grandchildren, about the lessons and wisdom of my life that I hoped to somehow pass along to them. But these papers you wrote all seem rather cold and impersonal. They seem to be strictly about the money. In fact, if I didn't know better, I would say that you probably just plugged our names into one of your forms."*

Wow, that was an awkward moment because he had nailed it. That's exactly what I had done. I'd simply taken their information, pulled out one our forms, plugged their names in, and then passed it off as something I'd created just for them.

I don't know if you've ever seen a lawyer tap dance, but there I was, dancing like crazy because he had put his finger on the truth. I just wanted him to sign the documents, write the check, and end the meeting. I guess I was good at the dance, because I calmed him down and he paid my fee and left.

But he left me very unhappy. His questions caused me to realize that I had not only let him and my other clients down but I was also letting myself down. I could see that I had become like a worker on an assembly line: grab a part, slap it on, screw it in, move on to the next one.

But that was not why I got into the business. I became an estate planner because I wanted to help people. I wanted to help people at a very deep level, to make their family ties stronger, to pass on the things that meant the most to them, to make sure the way they handled their money and their estate planning was a true reflection of what mattered most to them. And I realized I wasn't doing that. I wasn't even coming close.

So I looked around to see if I could find anyone else who knew how to do what I wanted to do. I was hoping to pattern my practice after theirs. Unfortunately, I couldn't find anybody who had a model I could follow, so I decided I would just have to figure it out for myself.

Thus began a journey that continues to this day of developing the processes, the tools, and the support systems that allow caring advisers to address the deepest issues in their clients' lives. The result of that search is my company SunBridge and the SunBridge Legacy Builder Network, together with all the other practical tools, training, and support we provide for caring advisers.

How Do You Use The New Me Story?

It is important that The New Me Story be brief. Typically, you want to take no more than three minutes to tell the whole story. Thus, it has to move quickly. You don't go into a lot of detail, but there must be enough detail that prospective customers can relate to you.

The structure of The New Me Story is quite simple. There are four steps. *Step one* is to describe "*the old me.*" You briefly tell about the way you used to be, setting up the transformation that will soon follow in the story.

Going back to my example above, I gave you some background about who I used to be before my transformation. I shared that I had worked at the trust department, that I launched my own business, that I had become fairly successful. Thus you were able to see me and see the setting in which I was operating. It's important to build that foundation first, because people need to know you and be able to identify with the person who is "the old me."

Once you set the stage so that prospective customers can appreciate who you used to be, *step two* is "*the transforming event.*" Something happened that rattled your world. In my case, it was a customer challenging me on the quality of my work as it related to the connectedness of his life to the estate plan I had created. He was basically calling me out. That's a transforming event because it upset my world and I had to deal with it.

A transforming event is something that shakes up the status quo. Sometimes it may be a major earth-shattering, life-changing event like a major disaster, a serious illness, or perhaps even the death of a loved one. On the other hand, it may be something more subtle, something cumulative that has built up over time, like the feeling that enough is enough, that you've put up with this for too long and you've finally reached the breaking point. Sometimes, it's the last straw.

But whether it's large and dramatic, or small but irritating, it must create a pressure or tension that is understandable to the listener. It must be something that puts the protagonist of the story in a bind and creates a stress that cannot be ignored.

Step three is called "*the response,*" which is the way you react to the transforming event. It's usually more interesting in telling a story if you initially are not very positively inclined toward the transformation called for by the transforming event. Notice that in my example, my first reaction wasn't very admirable. I initially wanted to dance around the issue. I wanted the customer to write the check and be happy and be gone. I didn't want to be forced to make the changes the situation created. So a little bit of storytelling tension developed: would I change or would I just keep trying to dance around and avoid the issue?

It makes a more interesting story if the protagonist (which in this case is you as you're telling The New Me Story) initially pushes back, reacts badly, doesn't handle well the change that has been thrown his way. In telling this story about yourself, you may be inclined to present yourself only in the most positive light. But it's important that you share that slightly unsavory side of yourself, because it shows you to be more human. As humans, we resist change. Everybody wants things to be better but nobody wants to change.

If something happened that called for your change and you simply went along with it without even a pushback, that wouldn't sound very normal or credible. Prospective customers need to hear that you initially resisted; that's the natural, human thing to do. But then your better self took over and you came to realize, *"Hey, there is a call to action here and I need to take advantage of the situation."*

That's what happened to me. After the client left and I reflected on what he said, I realized this event was telling me I had been letting myself and my customers down, and a marvelous opportunity to make a major shift was presenting itself. As it turned out, that small event was the start of a significant journey for me, a journey that led to my becoming quite a different person.

And that leads to *step four,* *"the new me."* As a result of the way you respond to the transforming event, you have become someone who's different and much better qualified to help prospective customers address their concerns and problems.

Here's a brief review. *Step one is the old me.* This is who you used to be before the transforming event occurred. *Step two is the transforming event.* Something happened that rattled your world. *Step three is the response.* This is the way you initially resisted change, and then became a better, more qualified, competent person after your better self took over. *Step four is the new me.* As a result of your response to the transforming event, this is who you are now; someone who is much more capable of helping prospective customers solve their problems.

Telling the New Me Story

— The Old Me

— The Transforming Event

— The Response, Bad and Good

— The New Me

What Are Some Tips for Using The New Me Story?

The New Me Story may appear in a number of variations. It's possible you may have several different New Me Stories. The one you use will depend on the person or group to whom you are speaking.

It may also be called by many different names. Some people call it "Our Firm's Story" or "The Philosophy of My Practice."

It may vary in length. In some cases, such as when a physician is meeting with a prospective patient, the story may need to be substantially shorter than three minutes. In other cases, such as when you are speaking to a large group for an extended period, the story can be a little bit longer.

Regardless of how long you take or what name you give it, it is imperative that the story arc structure be preserved. The essence of the story is that you are different, and you are different because you have changed. You used to be typical—which is code for the way your competitors presently are—but something happened to you and you are now different, improved in your ability to deliver what your prospective customers need from you.

The best way to lose a sale is to be ordinary. The best way to be stuck with low fees is to be just like everybody else in the marketplace.

The New Me Story is a key ingredient, along with The How We Do It Story, for setting you apart from your competition and establishing value in the minds of your potential customers.

How Do You Create The New Me Story?

Creating The New Me Story is a rather interesting process. You use the same four steps as in telling the story, but you approach them in a different order when you are creating the story.

The first thing you must get clear about is how the story will end, or in other words, what does the "new me" look like? Remember Steven R. Covey's book, *The Seven Habits of Highly Effective People?* One of those seven habits is "begin with the end in mind." That's exactly what you do here.

To create the story, you start with *step number four*, the new me. Here's the question you must answer for yourself: "*What kind of person do I need to be at the end of the story so that I am seen by prospective customers as capable and qualified to help them solve their problems? Who is the new me?*"

In the story I told, the new me is someone who has wrestled with the issue of how to bring the human side of the customer's life into the planning process, someone who has gone to the trouble of creating systems and tools that allow caring advisors to connect with the real issues in client families. Because of who I have become, the new me is now more qualified to help estate planners and other advisors who seek to transform their practices and become more capable of dealing with the deep issues relating to the things that matter most to their clients.

Now you must ask the same question of yourself: "*What do my customers need from me? How have I become a better source of help to those customers than someone else who has not undergone the same transformation I have experienced?*"

Thus, the first step in creating the story of who you are is actually the end piece. Who are you today and how is it that you are now better able to help this person who's listening to your story?

The next phase in creating the story is to go back to *step number two,* the transforming event. Go back in your memory bank and find an event that was part of the chain of causation for your becoming the new you. In reality, you weren't changed by one single event. In fact, there are probably lots of events that contributed to your transformation. But for purposes of keeping the story short and simple, you need to identify one single event that was interesting and catalytic and capable of spurring the change. In other words, you're looking for one significant and credible trigger that caused you to change. It is important that it is believable and understandable to your prospective customers.

When I tell my story to professionals like estate planners and financial advisors, they understand and relate to my transforming event because they've probably had something like that happen in their work with their clients. They can appreciate how threatening it would be for a client to challenge you and call into question your client service process and your whole approach to planning. They can relate to the sense of failure a caring professional might feel when he realizes he's not living up to his own ideals.

Similarly, your transforming event must be something that really happened to you and to which your prospective customers can relate. It needs to be something your prospective customers can readily recognize as a life-altering experience, something of such impact that it is capable of causing the change you are describing.

After you determine how you want to be perceived by your prospective customers (the new you), and you identify an event that was a trigger or a catalyst for your becoming who you are today (the transforming event), the next piece in creating The New Me Story is

step number three, your response to the transforming event. Once you've identified the transforming event, you need to recall your reaction to it. You should look for your initial resistance to doing the right thing, especially your reluctance to change. Then consider how your better side took over and you transformed yourself in a positive way.

In an effective New Me Story, your reaction and response to the transforming event must be believable. In real life, change takes time and effort. Thus, as you construct the story, you need to describe your resistance and you need to allow the listeners to see the transformation process unfolding within the story. They need to see that you initially resisted but then the better side of your nature took over and you started to shift. It took some time, it wasn't overnight or magical but you did it, and here you are today, a better person because of it.

The final phase in creating The New Me Story is actually *step number one* when you're telling the story: who you used to be before the transforming event, before this change happened. The Old Me needs to be a sympathetic person that prospective customers can identify with, or at least find interesting. You need to have something going on in your life that makes you noteworthy, so prospective customers will be motivated to listen to the story.

So, to review, you <u>tell</u> the story, step one, step two, step three, then step four. You start by describing The Old Me, that is, who you were before. Next, you tell about The Transforming Event, and then you describe your response to the event, both the negative and the positive. Finally, you describe who you are today, someone more capable of helping prospective customers.

By contrast, you <u>form</u> the story or create the story by thinking through step four, then step two, then step three, then step one. That is, first identify who you are today. Identify those attributes you want to emphasize to prospective customers. That's the New Me. Then describe which event in your life played a key role in helping you become the New Me. After that, focus on how you responded to the Transforming Event, both negatively and positively. Finally, clarify who you used to be before the transformation.

Creating the New Me Story

— The New Me

— The Transforming Event

— The Response, Bad and Good

— The Old Me

How Do You Get Started Using The New Me Story?

As I mentioned, this story has to be brief. Prospective customers are typically only going to allow you about three minutes—and that's if it's an interesting story. They're often thinking that they came to this meeting to talk about their issues, not listen to you talk about yourself. Because brevity is so important, you need to do a certain amount of polishing before you start using this story with prospective customers.

I suggest that you start by writing down the positive characteristics you want to project to your prospective customers: Who are you and what makes you uniquely qualified to help them?

Next, write down what changed you. Go back in your memory and think about which events are causes for your becoming a new kind of a person. You'll be surprised at how many triggers there could have been. Find one that's interesting, that has a human believability about it. If it's big and dramatic, that's good. If it's only small but believable, that's still okay because we know that even small things can drive us to make major changes.

Think about and write down how you initially reacted and then how you ultimately changed in response to the event you identified. Finally, write a description of who you used to be before this change occurred.

Once you've written out what your story looks like, it's important to start telling the story. You might start by telling it to yourself, maybe into a recorder for the first time or two. Then find a colleague, a friend, or family member who is willing to give you a listening ear and good feedback. Say to them, "I'm working on telling a story about how I've changed and I wonder if you would listen to this story and then give me your thoughts about how it sounded." Listen to what they say and learn from their feedback.

As you practice, remember a few important points: The story has to be believable. The story has to be interesting. The story has to be short. However, it doesn't have to be perfect before you tell it to prospective customers.

Once it's pretty good, the very best practice is simply telling it to customers and prospects and seeing how they respond. Over time, the story's going to get better and better as you learn which words to use to help your listeners visualize the events you are describing. Now you're on your way.

Chapter Summary

- The New Me Story makes you more human. Others can relate to you because they know that real people have to deal with challenges in a constantly changing world.

- When prospective customers see that you have experienced life in real terms, that you're not merely a figure head, a plastic person, somebody with a title, somebody with a bunch of letters behind your name, or just a salesperson, then they can relate to you as a real person.

- The New Me Story is a powerful way for others to connect with you. We feel connected to the people whose stories we have listened to and who have listened to our stories.

- In order to make it easier for your customers to share their experiences, you have to set the example. They have to hear some of the things that have happened in your life. You have to open up to them in a real way. Again, you can't dominate the time, so it's important to be brief in this story and at the same time completely authentic.

- Another benefit of The New Me Story is that it gives prospective customers permission and encouragement to make their own changes. We're asking them to make a transformation as well. Your New Me Story is a subtle and powerful way to say, *"I've changed, and it's okay for you to change too."* While the message will never be spoken by you in those terms, nonetheless it will be understood by prospective customers in those terms.

- Telling your story shifts the meeting to the right side of the brain, which makes it more natural for prospective customer to share their stories with you. By making prospective customers more intuitive and less skeptical, it dramatically increases the odds they will make the decision to move forward.

- Telling The New Me Story and making it real, interesting, vibrant, and brief is a wonderful way to engage the customer and make sure you have an opportunity to offer your wisdom, your insight, your services, and your solutions.

- To create your New Me Story, take the time to sit down and write it out, step by step, in this sequence: This is who I am today, this is what caused me to change, this is the experience I had as I was going through the change. This is who I used to be.

- Next, practice telling it with somebody safe: This is who I used to be, this is what happened to me that changed me, this is how it changed me, this is how it felt as I was changing, and as a result, this is who I am today. Listen to their feedback and then tell it again and again.

Chapter 8

The Who Are You Story

Key Points

> The Who Are You Story allows you to connect with prospective customers on a human-to-human basis.

> The Who Are You Story has three components: 1) Who are you as a person? 2) What is your experience in this area? 3) What brings you here today?

> The three keys to a successful Who Are You Story are authentic curiosity, good listening skills, and a sense of purpose and direction.

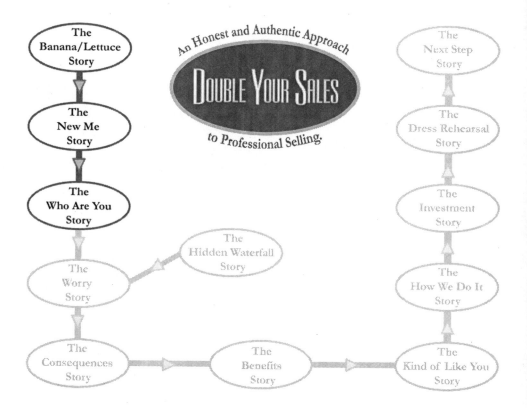

The Banana/Lettuce Story

The New Me Story

The Who Are You Story

The Worry Story

The Hidden Waterfall Story

The Consequences Story

The Benefits Story

The Kind of Like You Story

The How We Do It Story

The Investment Story

The Dress Rehearsal Story

The Next Step Story

An Honest and Authentic Approach

DOUBLE YOUR SALES

to Professional Selling.

What is The Who Are You Story?

The Who Are You Story is told by prospective customers, not by you. Your role is to provide the questions that act as a catalyst for your prospective customers to tell you about themselves, and for you to listen attentively. I call these kinds of questions "story-leading questions." Story-leading questions make it easy for customers to share experiences from their lives.

The Who Are You Story allows prospective customers to introduce themselves to you and to share meaningful aspects of their history and life experience with you. The Who Are You Story prepares prospective customers to describe the problems and concerns that have caused them to meet with you.

If you were to diagram The Who Are You Story, you would see that it looks something like a funnel, moving from general questions about prospective customers such as "How long have you lived here?" or "How did the two of you get together?" through a description of their experiences with the types of products or services you offer, and finally narrowing to the specific narrative of what brings them here today.

What is the Purpose of The Who Are You Story?

The purpose of The Who Are You Story is to create authentic sharing with prospective customers on a human-to-human level. This story also serves to move the sales meeting squarely to the right side of the prospective customers' brains. In addition, it uncovers important information you will need to have to be able to work effectively with these prospective customers.

A significant purpose for The Who Are You Story is to start building a sense of personal connection with the prospects you expect to become your customers. Narrating meaningful aspects of our life experience is a sure-fire way to create a human connection with another person. It is human nature to feel close to those people who listen attentively and authentically to our stories. When you create an environment in which prospective customers can share important information from their lives, you allow this powerful bonding process to begin.

When you genuinely and generously listen to prospective customers' Who Are You Stories, you let them see you are interested in them as people and not merely as customers. You communicate to them you are authentically interested in who they are and what makes them tick.

What Does The Who Are You Story Sound Like?

Some years ago, I was invited to the home of Dr. and Dr. Brown, two physicians with two darling young sons. After I laid out the proposed agenda for the meeting and they concurred, and after I shared with them my New Me Story, I steered the conversation into The Who Are You Story. It went something like this (names and details changed to protect confidentiality):

> *Advisor:* "I'm curious how two physicians ended up being married to each other. How did the two of you get together?"
>
> *Husband:* "That's easy, we met in medical school at the University of Florida. We had several classes together, and over time, we found ourselves more and more attracted to each other. We dated off and on for the first year or so, and then seriously during the last part of medical school. We were married shortly after graduation."

Advisor: "So, Mary, was there an immediate attraction? Was it love at first sight?"

Wife: "Well, I must admit that I thought he was strikingly handsome, but I didn't like his attitude at first. I thought he was kind of arrogant, so no, it wasn't love at first sight. There was not an immediate attraction."

Husband: "For me, I knew right away this was a woman I wanted to spend my life with, which was kind of funny because I wasn't even looking for a serious relationship. I had my mind strictly focused on getting through medical school. But all that changed the minute I met her. It just took a little time for her to get to know the real me."

Wife: "Because of his kindness and his persistence, I realized over time I was wrong in my initial assessment, that he really does have a big heart, and he loves people. That's what makes him a good doctor, and what makes him a good husband and father. But I try not to give him a big head."

Advisor: "It must've been challenging to deal with the courtship and then an engagement in the middle of medical school. How did you manage that?"

Wife: "I think it worked for us because we had similar priorities. We wanted to excel professionally, of course, but we also were committed to maintaining some semblance of balance in our lives. We had both seen family members who ended up hurting their families by spending too much time working. And it helped that we both understood what each other was going through."

Husband: "That's right, we both wanted to be great physicians, but not at the expense of not having a life. I think our core values have always been aligned that way.

Advisor: "That's really admirable. I meet a lot of couples who don't have that kind of clarity and alignment of values. Thanks for the insight.

"So after medical school, did you do your residencies in the state of Florida?"

Husband: "No, we did our residencies in North Carolina. Chapel Hill. That was a bit tricky, getting residencies for both of us in the same town. On that score, we had to be pretty flexible, but in the end, we were very fortunate."

Wife: "We would have loved to have residencies here in Florida, because that's where we wanted to come back to, but we had to take the offers that were available. But as soon as we finished our residencies, we moved back here. This is where we wanted to raise our family."

Advisor: "Speaking of family, please tell me little bit about your sons."

Husband: "Our older son Marcos is seven. He's smart and very driven for someone his age. He's a real competitor, both at school and in sports. Our younger son is Tom. Tom is five and he is very curious about animals and nature and the environment. I have the impression he's going to be a great scientist one day.

Wife: "For brothers, they get along well with each other, and we love spending time together as a family. Obviously that's a challenge, since both of us have very busy practices. But we've been talking lately about cutting back on the number of hours I work each week."

Husband: "Please keep that confidential, because we haven't talked to my wife's partners about our ideas yet."

Advisor: "No problem. In fact, everything we say here tonight is confidential. And speaking confidentially, I'm curious about what experience either of you have had with estate planning. Have you ever prepared wills or trusts or anything like that before?"

Husband: "When Marcos was born, we went to the clinic at the law school, which was near the hospital where I was a resident, and had them prepare very simple wills. That was nearly seven years ago, and we haven't done anything since."

Wife: "I've been after my husband for years, saying we needed to update things since we live in Florida now and have a house and a significant income, but it just seems like life is so busy."

Advisor: "You must have discussed estate planning with your financial advisor, John, because he's the one who recommended you see me."

Husband: "We did mention it to him, but he said you were the expert on that subject, so we didn't get into it very much with him."

Advisor: "Well, I'm curious about why, after nearly seven years, you decided now is the time to look into this. What in the world is triggering your decision to focus on your estate planning now?"

Wife: "Hawaii. We're taking a trip to Hawaii in about two weeks, and I'm afraid to get on the airplane together with my husband without having some planning in place."

Husband: "I've told her that nothing is going to happen . . . ."

Wife: "And I know that, in my head, but in my heart, I don't want to leave our two sons here alone without making sure we've planned for them."

Husband: "It is something we definitely need to do. We know that. So this second honeymoon trip we're taking provides a good excuse to get this done now.

How Do You Use The Who Are You Story?

For most professionals who sell for a living (and isn't that all of us?), The Who Are You Story will feel very natural. After all, we do what we do because we enjoy people. The Who Are You Story is a wonderful opportunity to get to know them and understand their concerns.

Because most people enjoy talking about themselves, most prospective customers will likewise feel comfortable telling their own Who Are You Story. However, because many of the professionals they worked with in the past may have been "all business," they may be skeptical that you are authentically interested in them and their story. For this reason, it is important that during The Banana/Lettuce Story you tell them you will be asking them to share with you a little bit about themselves as background for your work together.

It is also important, as you move into The Who Are You Story, that you provide a customer-centered explanation for getting to know them personally. This explanation must be genuine and credible, or the prospective customers will feel that you are simply manipulating them for your own purposes. A long, drawn-out explanation is not required; a sentence or two of explanation is usually sufficient, so long as the explanation is from the customers' perspective and not just yours. It might sound something like this:

> "I've found over the years that each customer who comes to me has a unique and interesting background that ultimately plays a large part in our decision to work together. Do you mind if I ask you a few questions about your background? I've found this helps me understand the context in which your concerns have originated."

I like to think of The Who Are You Story as a dance, not a march. I lead, but I do not dictate the steps that my partners (the prospective customers) will use. There is certain territory I want to cover, but I must pay careful attention to them and the music inside their heads in order to be successful.

Over the years, I have discovered several good story-leading questions to help launch or move forward good Who Are You Stories from prospective customers. Here are some I like:

- So, Mr. and Mrs. Smith, how did you two get together?
- Where did you grow up and how did you end up here in Florida?
- Have you always lived here in Orlando, or did you move here from somewhere else?
- What kind of work do you do, and how did you get started in that field?
- Please tell me a little bit about yourself and your family.
- Did you grow up in one place or did you move around a lot?
- Have you always wanted to be a _____?
- How did you first meet your spouse?

- If you didn't live here in _____, where do you think you might live instead?
- What do you like most about the work you do?
- What kind of people do you most enjoy being around?
- What would you say has been the most satisfying era of your life up until now?
- What do you like to do when you're not working?
- Who are some people in your life who went out of their way to lend you a helping hand?

After posing your initial questions, you should ask appropriate follow-up questions, based on the stories the prospective customers are telling you. The key ingredient here is your own boundless curiosity. If you genuinely care for people and want to know who they are and what makes them tick, you will find good follow-up questions come very naturally. It's simply the art of a caring conversation.

Once you have acquired a sense of who these people are and you have an understanding of their background, you'll want to start nudging the conversation into an exploration of their experience working in your field. Depending on your area of expertise, these questions might sound something like the following:

- I'm curious, Mr. and Mrs. Jones, about your experience in the world of investments. What can you tell me about that?
- Will this be the first home you've bought together?
- Have you ever done any estate planning before? What was that experience like for you?
- What kind of car-buying experiences have you had in the past?
- What is the current status of your long-term planning?
- What experiences, good or bad, have you had working with insurance agents in the past?
- Is this the first time you've considered doing any cosmetic surgery?

This particular phase of The Who Are You Story will provide you enormously vital information about their experiences and attitudes. If you listen carefully to their answers to these questions, you can avoid a number of future traps and minefields.

The final phase of The Who Are You Story is what I call the "What Brings You Here Today Story." This part of the story will help launch into the next story in the Double Your Sales process, The Worry Story.

The fact that these prospective customers are sitting and talking with you today is a reflection of their sense that something is not quite right in their lives, and you may be the person who can help them make it right. Something is troubling them, otherwise they would be at work or out doing something else like playing golf or getting a root canal. Your job is to ask the right questions that help you, and them, understand what brought them to see you at this particular point in their lives.

What Are Some Tips for Using The Who Are You Story?

I have found that there are three key ingredients to success with this story: authentic curiosity, good listening skills, and a sense of purpose and direction.

Authentic curiosity will motivate you to communicate your interest in the prospective customers and their lives. It will allow you to hear their answers with a genuine sense of delight in getting to know them as fellow human beings. It will cause you to want to know more, and then ask the next question, and the next, and the next. Authentic curiosity will show up readily, and will be easily apparent to prospective customers. If it's not authentic, they will sense that too. They will inherently know if this is only a sales gimmick on your part.

Good listening skills will help steer the conversation. Attentive listening will make sure that the next question you ask, and the one after that, make sense and follow naturally from what they have already told you.

Good listening skills will also help you glean invaluable information from the stories they are telling you. The Double Your Sales process requires that you be something of a detective, with the ability to identify clues and important tidbits of information as you converse with prospective customers.

Your use of good listening skills also makes it easier for prospective customers to open up their life stories to you, because they will feel appreciated and understood.

Having a sense of purpose and direction is also essential. At first glance, The Who Are You Story may appear to be merely idle cocktail party chatter. Not so. This is learning about them with attention and purpose. The Who Are You Story will guide prospective customers to the place where both of you ultimately want to go: a discussion of their concerns and worries.

As described above, there are three major components of The Who Are You Story. First, "Who are you as a person?" Second, "What is your experience in this field?" Third, "What brings you here today?" By the end of The Who Are You Story, you should have rich and meaningful answers to these questions as they pertain to these prospective customers.

At the same time, it is important that this conversation be allowed to evolve naturally and comfortably. Remember, this is a dance, not a march. Allow the stories and the relationship to blossom.

Yet it is also important to keep in mind that this dance does not last forever. Early on in my experience using customers' stories in the sales process, I found myself listening endlessly to prospective customers, who loved telling their stories. At the end of our meeting, they appreciated having someone to listen to their experiences, but I had not been focused on moving them toward a decision whether to work with me or not. Balance, I soon learned, is the key. You must learn to balance your interest in their stories with your purpose for the meeting, which is to discover whether there is a basis for working together.

How Do You Create The Who Are You Story?

I have found the best way to create The Who Are You Story is to have a small number of story-leading questions that feel comfortable and natural for you. Several that I like to use are listed above. As you read my list, others may also come to your mind.

It's not necessary to have a vast number of story-leading questions. Half a dozen that work for you will be plenty. Remember, these questions are used to initiate the conversation. Once they tell their first story, you'll be on your way, dancing with the prospective customers, asking questions as your curiosity directs, and moving through the three phases of the question.

How Do You Get Started Using The Who Are You Story?

I've found that almost any social setting lends itself to practicing The Who Are You Story. Just about any time you are around people will work: cocktail parties, meetings at church, in the line at the grocery store. Any time you have the occasion to be around someone you don't know very well, you can practice your story-leading questions and your attentive listening. For most of you, this will be very natural.

When you start using The Who Are You Story in a sales situation, the main things to remember are to move with direction and purpose while at the same time balancing the human side of the conversation. Keep in mind the three components of The Who Are You Story. Remember that your ultimate aim is to connect on a human-to-human level so you have a chance to go to the next story, The Worry Story.

Chapter Summary

- The Who Are You Story is an opportunity to get to know prospective customers on a human level and to give them the opportunity to introduce themselves to you.

- The Who Are You Story effectively moves the entire sales meeting to the right side of the brain, where buying decisions are made.

- The Who Are You Story can be launched with a small handful of story-leading questions, followed up by additional questions as directed by your curiosity.

- The Who Are You Story has three important components: First, "Who are you as a person?" Second, "What is your experience in this field?" Third, "What brings you here today?"

- The three keys to a successful Who Are You Story are: 1) genuine curiosity, 2) attentive listening, and 3) a sense of direction and purpose.

Chapter 9

The Worry Story

Key Points

➤ In The Worry Story, your prospective customers share with you the concerns that led them to come to see you.

➤ In most cases, you should seek to uncover several substantial worries, or at least one very large one for which you can offer solutions.

➤ Unless prospective customers have significant worries they are willing and able to share with you, you probably don't have a customer.

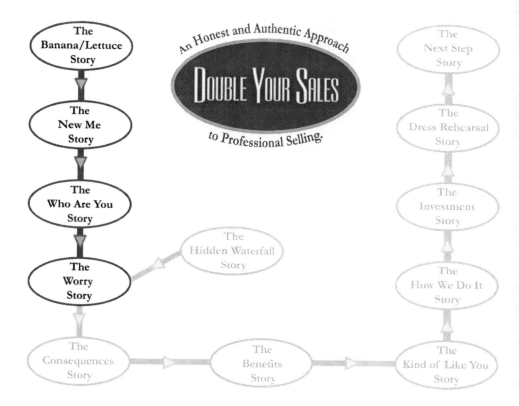

The Banana/Lettuce Story → The New Me Story → The Who Are You Story → The Worry Story → The Hidden Waterfall Story

An Honest and Authentic Approach DOUBLE YOUR SALES to Professional Selling.

The Next Step Story → The Dress Rehearsal Story → The Investment Story → The How We Do It Story → The Kind of Like You Story

The Worry Story → The Consequences Story → The Benefits Story → The Kind of Like You Story

What is The Worry Story?

The Worry Story is your prospective customers' expression of their concerns and what lies behind those concerns. The Worry Story usually follows quite naturally from The Who Are You Story, especially the segment that explains what brought them to see you today.

The Worry Story is told by your prospective customers, usually in response to your story-leading questions. It is essential that prospective customers articulate their worries themselves; it doesn't count if you try to tell them what their worries are.

Your prospective customers may only have one very large, compelling worry, but often they are troubled by several concerns. The Double Your Sales process is more successful if you can help them identify multiple worries. Human nature is such that it is easy to dismiss a single worry, even a large and frightening one, but it is more difficult to dismiss several clustered worries.

What is the Purpose of The Worry Story?

The purpose of The Worry Story is to help your prospective customers articulate their needs and concerns. This helps them appreciate the seriousness of their problems, which helps increase the value of the solutions you will provide. It also helps you determine whether you are the right person to help them address their concerns.

The Worry Story can also help you uncover additional issues that may be troubling the prospective customers. This creates an opportunity for you to propose a larger, more comprehensive, and hence more valuable solution.

What is an Example of The Worry Story?

The Worry Story is told by the prospective customers in response to your thoughtful questions. It might sound something like this:

Advisor: Thank you for sharing with me more about who you are and what your background is. Obviously you're here today because something is on your mind. Would you mind sharing with me the concerns that led you to come here today?

Husband: We are primarily concerned about the safety of our retirement plan assets. There's been so much in the news lately about people losing a large chunk of their retirement funds because of poor investments.

Advisor: That's a topic that has lots of people on edge these days. Would you mind sharing with me more specifically what you are worried about?

Wife: What worries me the most is that a lot of my husband's retirement plan is invested in the stock of the company he works for. It's always been a good company, but I've seen a lot of other good companies get into financial trouble and their employees were left not only without a job but without any retirement security.

Advisor: Did that happen to someone you know personally, Mrs. Brown, or is it something you've read about?

Wife: It actually happened to my co-worker's brother who lives in another part of the country, but she was worried sick about him. That made me stop and think we need to look more closely at my husband's retirement plan.

Advisor: And do you share that concern, Mr. Brown?

Husband: Yes, that does bother me, and I'm also concerned whether my current advisor has put any risky mortgage-backed securities into my portfolio. There's a lot of stuff on my retirement plan statements that we just don't understand.

Advisor: So what happens when you receive your statements?

Husband: Well, I can tell whether it's gone up or down, and I can recognize a lot of things on there, but there's a whole bunch I don't know. And that makes me nervous.

Wife: I feel the same way. Our current advisor never was very good, it seems to me, at explaining things to us, and then when things started getting rocky in the market, we almost never heard from him except form letters he sent out trying to reassure us. It was pretty obvious to me that he was as scared as we were. But I expect my advisor to stay in touch with us and let us know what's going on.

Advisor: And do you have similar concerns about your current advisor, Mr. Brown?

Husband: Maybe not as much as my wife, but I do feel that he let us down when times got a little sticky.

Advisor: Mrs. Brown, are there any other concerns you have you would like us to discuss today?

Wife: No, I think that's it.

Advisor: And you, Mr. Brown? Is there anything else you're worried about?

Husband: If we could address those issues, that would be great with me. I think that's all.

Advisor: So, if I've heard you correctly, you mentioned several things that are troubling you. First, you expressed you are afraid you may have too much of your own company's stock in your retirement plan. Second, you're not sure if you have any mortgage-backed securities in your portfolio and you would be concerned if you did. And the third thing I heard was you feel your current advisor doesn't do a very good job educating and informing you and doesn't stay in touch with you when market conditions get rough. Did I hear that right?

Wife: Yes, that's a pretty good summary.

How Do You Use The Worry Story?

You use The Worry Story at the end of The Who Are You Story to discover the concerns your prospective customers want to address. Usually, the final segment of The Who Are You Story, which focuses on the story of why they are here today, segues naturally into The Worry Story. Sometimes, without your asking any additional questions, prospective customers will tell you what they're worried about in explaining why they are there to see you.

If prospective customers don't automatically tell you their primary concerns as part of The Who Are You Story, then you should coax them to do so by asking gentle, thoughtful questions, as demonstrated in the above example. If prospective customers have initiated the meeting, it should not be difficult for them to state the concerns that initially caused them to come to see you.

In some cases, prospective customers may be meeting with you as a favor to another advisor or for some other reason besides their own initiation of the process. In those cases, they may be unclear about what concerns you can help them with and therefore what concerns they should mention to you. When that happens, it is often helpful to describe some of the reasons for which other people in similar circumstances have come to meet with you. Your attentive listening during The Who Are You Story will provide you clues on how to suggest concerns they may have.

One common mistake that salespeople make at this juncture is to assume that if prospective customers identify one humongous worry, they don't need to probe for more. Sometimes one great big worry is sufficient to make a sale and engage the customer. Nevertheless, I think it is wise to try to discover as many areas of concern as possible.

The larger the number and weight of worries prospective customers have shared with you, the greater the likelihood you will be able to show them added value in your solutions. This will make it more likely they will engage you, and it will make it more likely the engagement will be for a larger purpose.

My general rule of thumb when meeting with prospective customers is to look for at least three or four solid and substantial concerns. There may be one huge concern that is pushing them to see me now, but almost always there are others orbiting nearby. Focusing on the whole bundle of concerns will add value to the engagement and will make it easier to successfully close the sale. Multiple lines of value create greater sales potential and larger sales.

Once prospective customers have shared their worries, it is useful and appropriate to restate those concerns back to them in your own words. This helps to confirm to them they have been heard and understood, or if you did not hear or understand them accurately, it helps to clear up any miscommunication.

What Are Some Tips for Using The Worry Story?

One of the best ways to prepare to use The Worry Story is to make a list of up to 10 to 12 worries and concerns that your products or your services can address. You have a number of issues for which you can provide valuable solutions. Making a list of them not only helps you get clear about how you help people, it helps you verbalize the value you and your company deliver to your customers.

Try this exercise yourself. What are 10 to 12 worries or concerns that you and your company help your customers address?

1]

2]

3]

4]

5]

6]

7]

8]

9]

10]

11]

12]

For many professionals who sell, creating this list is very affirming. This exercise reinforces the idea that you have significant value to offer your customers. You can see that you have wide-ranging capabilities that may not be recognized at first glance. You are able to see that the topics and areas of concern you can address frequently have significant financial and/or emotional impact. Nearly everyone who completes this simple exercise comes away with a new appreciation for the value they and their company provide to others.

Having this list in mind will help you as you meet with prospective customers. It will help you formulate good story-leading questions that remind prospective customers of issues or concerns they may have forgotten to mention. Having the list in mind also increases your confidence, which is a big factor in successfully using the Double Your Sales process.

One critical point in creating a good Worry Story is the rule that it is okay to ask prospective customers if something is a concern of theirs, but it is never acceptable to tell them directly what they should be worried about. It doesn't count if you say it; it only counts if they say it.

To say to prospective customers, "You should be worried about this and this and this," is not only a waste of time, but it also throws the entire Double Your Sales process off kilter. Unless prospective customers articulate their concerns and take ownership of them, even the most profound problems—from your perspective—will have no weight in moving prospective customers toward buying from you.

The correct way to invite prospective customers to recognize or acknowledge dangers or areas of concern of which they are unaware or refuse to own is to use a Hidden Waterfall Story, which is discussed in Chapter 10.

How Do You Create The Worry Story?

You create The Worry Story by taking The Who Are You Story all the way to its logical conclusion, which is the story of why they're here today, and by listening to the prospective customers' answers. Then you should ask story-leading questions that lead them to articulate their own personal concerns and issues. As with all the steps in the Double Your Sales model, this is a dance, not a march, and this particular portion of the process is a very gentle dance. It can never be forced.

Your list of the 10 to 12 problem areas you and your company can address will guide you into thoughtful story-leading questions, which will in turn help prospective customers recognize and reveal to you their personal areas of concern. Careful listening during The Who Are You Story will also provide clues and insights to help you form gentle yet effective story-leading questions.

How Do You Get Started Using The Worry Story?

To get started using The Worry Story, develop your list of 10 to 12 problems you can tackle. Then share your list with a professional colleague or family member who is familiar with your business and work together to refine your list and add to it. Ask them to also help you express the items on your list clearly and crisply. Learn how to describe those items in ways that resonate with your prospective customers.

When you're satisfied with your list, practice asking existing customers what concerns or worries they had when they first came to see you, and how your work together enabled them to address those worries or concerns. Learn to converse comfortably with them about how you create value for others. This will increase your confidence in the value of your service to your customers, and it will also help you learn which words and phrases connect best with your customers.

The types of worries and concerns you help your customers solve is your stock in trade. You've got to be able to talk about what you do from the perspective of problems solved for your customers, not in terms of the features of your products or services. When you can do that, you're ready to tackle The Worry Stories of real-life prospective customers.

Chapter Summary

- The Worry Story is a story told by prospective customers about the issues and concerns they believe you might be able to help them address.

- The Worry Story will usually flow naturally out of The Who Are You Story.

- The Worry Story is told by prospective customers in response to your gentle and thoughtful story-leading questions.

- One of the keys to asking good story-leading questions and hence to developing a good Worry Story from prospective customers is to create a list of problems and issues that you and your business are able to solve for your customers.

- The types of worries and concerns you help your customers solve is your stock in trade.

- When it comes to prospective customers' worries, it only counts if they believe it and they say it.

- When prospective customers believe they have problems and concerns you can help them with and when they share those problems and concerns with you, it creates an opportunity for you to deliver value by helping them solve those problems and concerns.

- When prospective customers will not own or acknowledge worries that seem obvious to you, it is inappropriate and counterproductive for you to tell them what they should worry about. In such a case, you should use a Hidden Waterfall Story to see if it will help them appreciate and take ownership of the dangers they face.

Chapter 10

The Hidden Waterfall Story?

Key Points

➤ The Hidden Waterfall Story is a story of somebody who messed up and as a result got into trouble.

➤ If prospective customers internalize The Hidden Waterfall Story, it will cause them to acknowledge a problem they don't recognize or own a problem they are denying.

➤ You should have a Hidden Waterfall Story for each of the 10-12 problems that you and your company can solve.

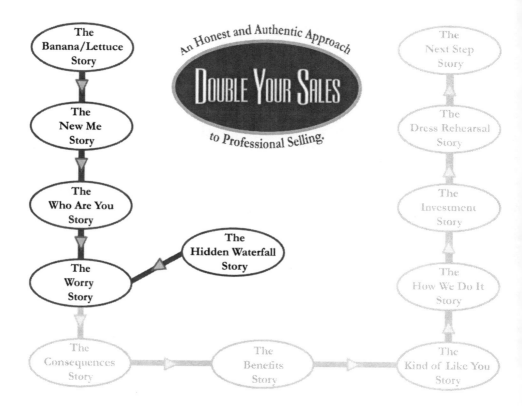

What is The Hidden Waterfall Story?

The Hidden Waterfall Story is a story from your personal experience, from the experience of a colleague, or from the life of a famous person about someone who made a serious mistake and, as a result, got into serious trouble.

The label "Hidden Waterfall Story" is a metaphor, much like The Banana/Lettuce Story. In this metaphor, you are an experienced river guide, and you are taking a group of inexperienced tourists on a kayaking trip. They are kayaking merrily down the middle of the river, unaware of the dangers that lurk ahead. Because of your experience, you understand those dangers. Your job is to warn them of the dangers and help them avoid the pitfalls.

In this particular stretch of river, although the water is smooth and flowing easily, you know that just around the next bend lies a 100 foot waterfall. If the kayakers do not change course quickly, the current will soon become so swift they cannot resist it and they will plunge over the waterfall to serious injury or even death.

Unfortunately, because it's such a pretty day and the river is so peaceful, and because they suspect your motives anyway, the tourists aren't inclined to listen to you or believe you. Simply telling them of the dangers isn't working. You must find a way to communicate with them so they will appreciate the serious danger they are in and take corrective action.

The solution is to tell them of *someone else* who failed to recognize or heed the dangers they faced and, as a result, suffered the painful consequences. That is what I call a Hidden Waterfall Story.

What is the Purpose of The Hidden Waterfall Story?

The purpose of The Hidden Waterfall Story is to teach your prospective customers to recognize dangers of which they are unaware, or to help them acknowledge the seriousness of dangers about which they are in denial.

Human nature being what it is, we often do not respond well to unpleasant information. When we receive unpleasant information in a lecture format or in an imperative mode, our tendency is to reject, deny, or minimize the information.

For example, if I were to tell prospective customers "You must do special planning to avoid the dangers of estate taxes," they may resist my directive for a wide variety of reasons.

- It may be a matter of misunderstanding; they simply don't realize how serious the danger is.
- It may be a matter of stubbornness; they resent being told what to do.
- It may be a matter of arrogance; they think they are smarter than I am.
- It may be a matter of suspicion; they think I'm just trying to raise my fees by selling them something they don't really need.
- It may be a matter of laziness or inertia; they see the problem but they just can't seem to get around to doing anything about it.

For these and any number of other reasons, *telling* prospective customers directly about the dangers they face may not move them to action. Instead, I need to invite them to action by using a story.

A story is often the most effective way to convey unpleasant information, for several reasons. A story is usually more understandable than a lecture. A story does not force information down the listener's throat. It is simply an account of what happened. Stories also carry their own third-party credibility. The veracity of the story stands largely on its own two feet, and is not solely dependent on the smarts or character of the one telling the story.

As a result, a Hidden Waterfall Story is usually the best way to help prospective customers learn about and appreciate the seriousness of a danger they face. It is often the best way to help prospective customers take ownership of a problem they recognize, but for which they are in denial as to the seriousness of the danger.

The Hidden Waterfall Story lets them own the problem, without compulsion, belittlement, or confrontation. In a sales setting, if you resort to any of those tactics, you may win the point, but you will certainly lose the match.

What is an Example of The Hidden Waterfall Story?

You should tell a Hidden Waterfall Story when you recognize a significant worry that your prospective customers ought to have, but which they are not mentioning or taking seriously. Here is an example.

> *Advisor:* When you shared with me the things that you are worried about, I was surprised you did not mention the threat of substantial estate taxes. That's often a serious concern for many of my clients. If not tended to, estate taxes can cause a massive amount of damage to your estate and to your surviving family.

> *Husband:* Well, I think that danger is overblown. Besides, I'll be dead and I won't have to worry about it.

Advisor: You could be right, but would you mind if I shared an experience I had early in my private practice in Mississippi?

Husband: Sure, go ahead.

Advisor: One of the first probate and estate settlement cases I worked on was a wonderful older lady from one of the town's most prominent families. She died with a relatively simple will that included no tax planning. I'm certain that before her death, neither she nor her family were aware of the seriousness of their oversight.

Her estate was not exceptionally large, in the range of $2.5 to $3 million. But because she had done no tax planning, besides her personal exemption, her estate was fully taxable at an average tax rate of almost 50%. The magnitude of her mistake became all too clear when the CPA prepared the estate tax return.

Have you ever held a check for $1,100,000? I have, and it was made payable to the Internal Revenue Service. I also held a smaller check payable to the Mississippi Department of Revenue. When the lady's son, who was her executor, handed me those checks to mail in with his mother's tax returns, his hands were literally trembling. Handing over that money to the IRS was one of the hardest things he ever had to do.

He and I had a conversation that day about the good that money could have done, had she only done proper tax planning. We talked about how much education for grandchildren and great-grandchildren that money could have paid for. We talked about the impact that money might have had if it had gone to her church, to the college she loved, and to other causes around the community she supported. We talked about how the family might have felt if the money had gone to people and organizations that his mother truly loved, instead of going for taxes. It was a touching conversation, one I will never forget and one that I hope I never have to repeat.

I'm curious, Mr. and Mrs. Smith. What stands out for you in that story?

Wife: I don't think I realized just how much money the IRS takes from us when someone dies.

Husband: I knew it was bad, but I assumed there's not much you can do about it.

Advisor: Would you mind if I explained in a bit more detail how the estate tax works in this country?

How Do You Use The Hidden Waterfall Story?

You may not need to use The Hidden Waterfall Story at all. If the prospective customers identify worries of their own, in sufficient numbers and with sufficient weight, you can just focus on those. If the ones they articulate will engender consequences and benefits significant enough to offset the heft of the price of your goods or services, you don't have to push them to identify additional worries.

On the other hand, if prospective customers are having trouble identifying and articulating sufficient worries of their own, or if they are unaware of or in denial of a major problem that you can see, you should use a Hidden Waterfall Story to help educate them of the dangers and help them take ownership of the problems.

When that is the case, you should gently raise the worry you think they ought to have and obtain permission to share an experience about that topic. Ideally, this will be an experience from your own life, based on your work with people in similar settings. However, if you do not have a good story of your own, it is nearly as effective for you to share the experience of a colleague. It is also effective in many cases to use examples from the lives of celebrities and other well-known people.

To tell a Hidden Waterfall Story effectively, you must provide sufficient detail to demonstrate that the story is true and to allow the listeners to picture the events as they unfold. An effective Hidden Waterfall Story invites prospective customers to re-create the narrative in their minds as they hear it from you. Their internalization of the story, based on their ability to visualize what happened, is the key to successfully changing their minds or re-educating them to add this particular concern to their list of significant worries.

After you have told The Hidden Waterfall Story, you should ask gentle questions to ascertain the impact of the story on them. You need to determine if they have accepted that worry or problem as their own. If so, then you can add it to the list of worries you will discuss later in The Consequences Story and The Benefits Story. Their answers may also indicate you need to provide them some additional education, in order that they have a sufficient understanding of the issue and the consequences and benefits that flow from it.

But what do you do if, after hearing The Hidden Waterfall Story, they continue to deny that this issue is something they are worried about? Put simply, you forget about it. You let it go.

You can only sell solutions to problems prospective customers acknowledge they have. Right or wrong, if they say they don't have a problem, that's the end of it. If it's not a problem for them, then for purposes of today's meeting, it's not a problem. You have to move on and focus on the problems they are willing to own.

(You forget about it, that is, for purposes of this sales meeting. If they become your customers based on other worries that they do acknowledge, in serving them you will still need to help them avoid the dangers you see they have.)

The Hidden Waterfall Story is a reality check, both for prospective customers and for you. It helps prospective customers get real about the dangers they face and about their willingness to own up to those dangers. If their lack of concern is due to a lack of information, it creates a teaching opportunity for you. If their lack of concern is based on their inability to face up to real dangers that confront them, it creates an opportunity for you to gently but effectively call their hand. Either way, it invites them to face reality.

The Hidden Waterfall Story is a reality check for you because it helps you know what issues and worries these prospective customers are actually concerned about. As much as you might want something to be a worry for them because you think it will help you make the sale, if The Hidden Waterfall Story fails to lead them to acknowledge and own that problem, then you have to face the reality that this particular worry will not help you in this sales meeting. If they don't own the problem, they won't buy your solution. It's now time for you to get real too.

What Are Some Tips For Using The Hidden Waterfall Story?

Hidden Waterfall Stories are directly correlated with the 10-12 problem areas that your products or services can effectively address. For each of those 10-12 problem areas, you need to have at least one good Hidden Waterfall Story about someone who messed up and bore the consequences of that mistake, either from your own personal experiences, the experiences of a colleague, or the mistakes of a famous person.

At this point, you should refer to the list you created in the previous chapter where you identified the 10-12 problem areas your products or services can address. For each of those problem areas, try to recall an occasion in which somebody screwed up, and consequently had to deal with the impact of that mistake.

How Do You Create The Hidden Waterfall Story?

Once you have identified these 10-12 examples of people making mistakes, you need to cultivate your ability to tell these stories artfully and authentically.

In telling these stories, you must relate sufficient context and detail that prospective customers can easily visualize the events as you describe them and sense that the story is true. It's what happens to the story once it gets inside their heads that matters most. Only if they internalize the story will it cause them to acknowledge a problem they don't recognize or own a problem they are denying.

It is important that the narrative include a vivid description of the impact of the mistake made by the person in the story. Sometime people make mistakes and somehow avoid the consequences of those mistakes. In The Hidden Waterfall Stories you tell, there must always be significant consequences.

You must pay attention to the way you lead in to a Hidden Waterfall Story. You need to raise the topic gently and ask the prospective customers' permission before sharing the story. Doing so will increase the likelihood that they will listen to the story and respond positively to it.

Similarly, the gentle questions you ask at the end of the story to discover whether they "got it" are essential to the effectiveness of your

Hidden Waterfall Stories. You should not go forward in your meeting until you know whether or not they acknowledge this particular worry as one of their own.

When you have identified the 10-12 Hidden Waterfall Stories you wish to add to your repertoire, there is no alternative except to practice, practice, practice. Once again, you will want to rely on family, friends, and associates to listen to your stories and to give you feedback. You can practice by yourself and you can practice in front of a mirror, but ultimately, good storytelling requires story listening. You need to have a live, attentive human being with whom you can rehearse your stories.

How Do You Get Started Using The Hidden Waterfall Story?

To get started using The Hidden Waterfall Story, return to your list of the 10-12 problems you can solve. For each one, identify a good example of someone who screwed up in that area and had to deal with the consequences. Then practice telling those 10-12 stories by yourself, with a safe listener, and eventually with prospective customers.

Chapter Summary

- The Hidden Waterfall Story helps prospective customers to understand dangers of which they are unaware or to take ownership of problems for which they are in denial.

- You do not need to use Hidden Waterfall Stories if prospective customers have themselves identified sufficient worries with sufficient weight.

- You must lead into a Hidden Waterfall Story by identifying the problem area the prospective customers have not raised, and by gently seeking their permission to tell an experience.

- This experience is about somebody who messed up, and as a result, paid a heavy price for their ignorance or mistake. This experience can be one of your own, one of your colleagues, or one of a famous person.

- You must lead out of a Hidden Waterfall Story with gentle questions that allow you to discover whether the prospective customers understood and accept the story, and thus own or acknowledge the problem area or worry.

- You should have a Hidden Waterfall Story that illustrates the dangers implicit in each of the 10-12 problem areas you can effectively solve with your products or services.

The Consequences Story

Key Points

> The Consequences Story is told by prospective customers as they imagine a future in which their worries and concerns have not been properly addressed.

> The Consequences Story invites prospective customers to take ownership not only of their problems but also of the failure to address their problems.

> The Consequences Story is one of the most important pieces of the Double Your Sales process because it drives home the dangers of not taking action. It is the antidote to one of your worst enemies: procrastination.

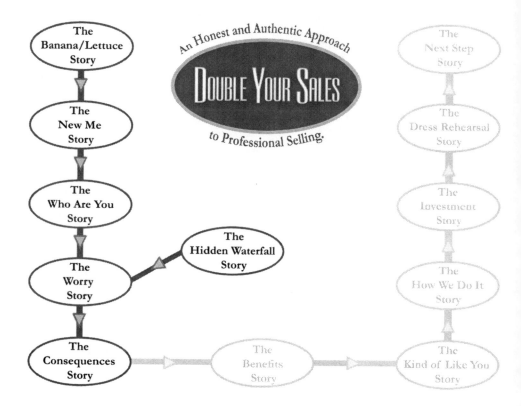

What is The Consequences Story?

The Consequences Story is a story told by prospective customers about the potential impact of their failure to properly address the worries and problems they have identified.

The Consequences Story is a narration of what the future might look like to prospective customers if they do not deal with their areas of concern. It is told in response to your story-leading questions, questions that invite them to look forward and picture what might occur if they fail to take action.

Typically, you will invite prospective customers to imagine and narrate a Consequences Story that addresses each of the worries or problem areas they have identified and that drills down into three or four levels of impact to themselves and those they love.

What is the Purpose of The Consequences Story?

One of the most powerful human motivators is our desire to avoid pain. If we can see that our behavior will hurt us or those we care about, we are likely to take action to avoid that injury.

The purpose of The Consequences Story is to help prospective customers recognize and anticipate the pain they will inflict on themselves and those they care about if they fail to find and implement appropriate solutions to the problems they have identified. The Consequences Story gives prospective customers a preview of the damage they will cause if they fail to take action and it motivates them to take steps to avoid that damage. It permits them to see and feel the impact of not working with you and implementing your answers and solutions.

In other words The Consequences Story helps prospective customers realize they cannot afford to procrastinate. Waiting and doing nothing are not viable options.

What is an Example of The Consequences Story?

Let's imagine a scenario in which an insurance agent is talking with a young husband and father named Bob about the need for life insurance. Bob has identified three worries or concerns he has: 1) If he dies, his wife will be thrust into the role of a single parent and will have to make hard choices about whether to go back to work full-time and how to afford household help and daycare services for their three young children. 2) If he dies, his wife will be left with a substantial unpaid mortgage on their home. 3) If he dies, his children may not be able to receive a quality education.

> *Agent:* Bob, you've shared with me three things you're worried about. Let's tackle each of them one at a time. The first one you mentioned was your fear that upon your death, your wife would be thrust into the role of a single parent and would not have the resources to either remain at home with your three children or to pay for household help and daycare services in case she chose to return to work. Did I understand that correctly?

> *Bob:* Yes, that's a pretty good summary of what I said.

> *Agent:* Well, Bob, let's try to imagine a time in the near future. For whatever reason, you chose not to do anything about life insurance, and then, heaven forbid, something happened to you. Your three children are still quite young and your wife is now a single parent. Not only does she have the cost of settling your affairs and paying for the funeral, but all the day-to-day pressures and bills still continue. To top that off, she's also right in the mid-

dle of the grieving process. If you were to imagine that situation, what would life look like for her if that were to happen?

Bob: I would say that life would look pretty bleak to her. She's normally pretty smart and levelheaded, but with that kind of stress on her, I'm not sure what kind of choices she might make. She and I have talked often about our priorities for giving our children our best attention, and she's chosen to cut back on her professional career while our children are younger, because of those priorities. But I'm afraid, with all those burdens, she might forget the importance of those priorities.

Agent: If you had to guess, what kind of choices do you think she might make in such a tough situation?

Bob: That's just it, none of her choices would be very good. Without financial resources, about the only choice she could make is to go back to work full time and look for some inexpensive way to cover childcare. Then she'd also have all of the responsibility of caring for the home and being a parent.

Agent: If that were to happen, how do you think it would affect her health and well-being?

Bob: As tough as she is, it would undoubtedly wear her down. It's hard to picture how she could operate very well for very long under those conditions.

Agent: And what do you imagine might be the impact on your children?

Bob: It would probably be even harder on them. They've lost their father, and in effect they've also lost their mother from a good part of their life. I don't like to even think about that.

Agent: I think I get the picture. Let's talk about your second area of concern, a large unpaid mortgage on your house. I get the impression that you would want your family to be able to stay in your home if something were to happen to you, but it sounds like you think your wife would not be able to pay the mortgage, given her earning capacity, even if she were working full time. Is that right?

Bob: That's right.

Agent: So if something were to happen to you, what is likely to happen with your home?

Bob: I think my wife would struggle for a while to stay in the house and try to make things work by using our savings, but after a few months, she would realize that she couldn't handle the house payments on her income. Sooner or later, she'd have to face up to the fact that she needed to sell the house and move to something smaller. That would be a tough decision for her.

Agent: Why do you say that would be a tough decision for her?

Bob: Because she really, really loves this house. We looked for a long time before we found it, and when we did, it was exactly what we were looking for. It's just right for our family. And she's put all kinds of work and love into this house. It's almost like it's become a part of her. So leaving here would be very emotional for her.

Agent: What do you think it would be like for her to tell the children they were selling the house and moving?

Bob: I imagine that she would put off telling them for as long as she could and then when she couldn't put it off any longer, it would be a very tearful day for everyone.

Agent: Which of your three children do you think would take it the hardest?

Bob: It would have to be our oldest daughter Julie. She loves the house and she especially loves the neighborhood and all her friends who live in the area. Her little group of girls loves to get together, they love to play in each other's back yards, and have sleepovers. They're almost inseparable. To leave that house in that neighborhood would almost break her heart.

Agent: I can tell that that would bother you a lot. Let's move on. Bob, you also mentioned a third area of concern, which is paying for your children's education. What would be the situation on that issue if you were to pass away in the near future?

Bob: It wouldn't be good, because we haven't really been able to put away a lot of money for the children's education yet.

Agent: So if suddenly you were gone as the breadwinner, would your wife likely be able to start saving for your children's college?

Bob: I think that would be highly unlikely.

Agent: Given that, what do you think might happen when your children started getting old enough for college?

Bob: They probably wouldn't have enough money for college. They could hope for scholarships, or maybe they could get student loans, or perhaps they could go to a lower quality school, but they sure couldn't get the kind of quality education I would like them to have.

Agent: And if that were to happen, how do you see that affecting their future?

Bob: I think they would really have to struggle. I think their odds of having financial success would be impaired. I think they would miss out on some of the important things of life, things I would like them to have.

Agent: And if you, as their father, were in a position to see all that, what would you be thinking?

Bob: I would think I had really let them down. I think one of the most important things parents need to provide their children is good education, and I would've dropped the ball.

Agent: Can you think of any other consequences if you were to die without sufficient life insurance?

Bob: I'm starting to think there are lots of them that never occurred to me before now.

How Do You Use The Consequences Story?

You use The Consequences Story to help prospective customers recognize and appreciate that the failure to act on their worries and concerns will produce real and painful consequences for themselves and those they love. The Consequences Story helps them take ownership of the ramifications of neglecting their problems.

To use The Consequences Story, you need to first make sure you understand their worries and what's behind those worries. As they tell their Worry Stories, you'll want to probe a little bit by asking questions like, "So, what makes that important to you?" or "Why does that matter to you and your family?"

Then in their Consequences Story, you need to help them take ownership of those problems, so the ramifications of not acting on those concerns become real to them. You need to invite them to imagine that the future has arrived and those problems have come home to roost. Now they're telling you what they see.

In that story, it's now the future, and their fears are being realized. They can see in their mind's eye that it's really happening. You want them to picture what it's doing to them and those they love; how it's affecting their own happiness and the happiness of those they care about most.

You do that with artful story-leading questions that allow them to project themselves into the future and from that future vantage point, imagine that the things they worried about are actually happening. For example, let's say their worry is about insufficient life insurance. Can you get them to picture their family trying to soldier on in a financial and emotional crisis? What's that going to do to the welfare and stability of the family? What's that going to do to the family home and their plans for the future? Can they picture themselves up there looking down and seeing their family struggling to deal with the consequences of their failure to increase their insurance coverage—what's that going to look like?

It is extremely important to remember that **The Consequences Story is their story, not yours.** You can tell them all day long, "You're going to leave your family in a real bind. Your family's going to lose their home. Your kids' opportunities for a quality education will be jeopardized." It may be completely true, but it doesn't mean much if it's just coming from you. Remember, you're the salesperson; your credibility is suspect because you're trying to sell them something.

It only counts if they say it. The question you have to consider is how to get them to envision the consequences to such a degree that they can tell you the story of what might happen to them. That's the key.

Sometimes, it doesn't take a whole series of story-leading questions to produce the desired effect. One advisor who has been using the Double Your Sales process for several years has found with many prospective customers, he simply has to ask, "What does it look like not to act in this area?" or "What does it look like not to solve or attempt to solve the problems you've shared with me today?" And then he just lets them talk about what comes to mind. He finds they are able to recognize and share with him the negative results of doing nothing, without much more prompting.

Similarly, as I worked with a group of cosmetic surgeons and taught them the Double Your Sales process, we learned all they had to say was something like "It sounds like the idea of addressing these concerns has been on your mind for a long time. I'm curious why you've finally said to yourself now is the time to do something about it?" Their prospective patients, it turns out, had been telling themselves The Consequences Story for quite some time. Thus, this simple inquiry allowed them to see and describe a future event (quite often in the very near future) in which they felt they needed to have taken action to address their concerns. A long and elaborate Consequences Story was not needed in that situation

What Are Some Tips For Using The Consequences Story?

You can make a sale only when the pain of leaving the problems unfixed plus the value of the benefits of fixing the problems outweigh the costs of fixing the problem. The Consequences Story adds weight to the "pain of leaving the problems unfixed" portion of this equation.

One of the things I've learned about the power of story is if a person tells a story with sufficient detail and attention, it affects them physiologically in the same way as if they were living through the actual event. That's true whether they're reliving a past occurrence or whether they're imagining something in the future that hasn't happened yet.

When you invite prospective customers to picture something in the future, and they are able to envision it and narrate that mental image back to you, even though it hasn't actually happened, in their minds it *is* happening. That makes it real. They see it in their heads and they feel it in their gut.

Having them verbalize the consequence is important. Sometimes they don't know what they know until they hear themselves say it. Saying it and hearing themselves say it makes it even more real.

So when they see it and they feel it and they say it and they hear it, all those senses combine to make it a real event for them. This process creates something concrete that can offset the very tangible cost of what it's going to take to fix the problem.

It is vital that you polish your skills in asking the story-leading questions that prompt them to tell their Consequences Story. That's because you're leading them to a place of great discomfort. One way to soften your questions is to wrap them in several hypothetical layers. It might sound like this: "So let's try to imagine, Mr. Black, that sometime in the future—now this is purely hypothetical of course—you've passed away and your family has lost both you and the earning capacity you represent. Now you're not going to be there, but try to picture in your mind's eye you're looking down and you're seeing all of this unfold"

By painting a hypothetical picture, you make it easier for prospective customers to go there in their imagination. They know it's not real, so they're more likely to accept the invitation to visit that place. But in the world of stories, even a visit to a hypothetical place is nearly as effective as a visit to a real place.

They have the ability to create images in their minds, and then by sharing stories about those images, those places become a new reality inside their heads. Once they're real in their heads, they become real to their gut. The discomfort they feel will drive them to do something. They feel it and now they've got to take action.

How Do You Create The Consequences Story?

Newcomers to this process occasionally encounter some common mental hurdles to using The Consequences Story effectively. One of these hurdles is the fear this will seem contrived to prospective customers, like you are following some kind of cheesy formula, like a clumsy psychotherapist asking, "And how would that make you feel?' And how would *that* make you feel?"

Once you start using this process, that concern will evaporate, for several reasons. First, because of your genuine interest in them and their stories, prospective customers will be fully engaged in the process by this stage of the meeting. It will feel quite natural and normal to them for you to want to investigate further their fears and concerns. Remember, they're now in intuitive mode, sharing stories with you.

Second, you will only rarely ask prospective customers a "feeling" question when you are exploring their Consequences Story. Instead, most of your story-leading questions will be "seeing" or "thinking" or "hearing" questions, which are safer and less intrusive for most people. Those questions sound like "What do you see when . . . " or "What comes to mind when . . . " or "What do you envision when . . . " or "What would it sound like if . . . ", as opposed to "How would you feel if . . . " You would use a "feeling" question only when the customers' own language suggested they would be inclined to go in that direction.

Third, in very short order, you'll find your story-leading questions will become artful and elegant, and totally conversational, not at all "therapeutic." They will flow from your authentic care and concern for these people, and your genuine curiosity about where their minds and imagination might take them. You just need to practice a bit and then trust your instincts. You will know when a question doesn't fit, and you will correct it or not ask it in the first place.

Another mental hurdle that newcomers to this process sometimes have is their reluctance to talk about unpleasant things, or to take prospective customers to an uncomfortable place. This is a natural reaction. None of us likes to be the bearer of bad news. I have learned, however, in more than 10 years of using this process myself and teaching and coaching others how to use it that such fear is unfounded.

If there is any discomfort involved in telling The Consequence Story, the prospective customers are creating it themselves. I have learned that no one will go beyond a point where they can't bear to go. Thus there is no danger that you will somehow inflict any kind of permanent damage. If you start to go too far, they will let you know.

Related to this issue of creating discomfort is the strict rule that you should not, at this stage of the meeting, try to "rescue" them or "save them from the pain" they may be experiencing. Whatever hurt they may have created for themselves needs to stay with them until, with The Benefits Story and The How We Do It Story, you show them that the way to avoid these undesirable consequences is to work with you through your solution process. Don't worry, you will get to be the knight in shining armor. You will ride to their rescue, but only at the right moment. Premature rescue will hobble your sales results.

How Do You Get Started Using The Consequences Story?

As has been recommended in previous chapters, it's a good idea to practice The Consequences Story with a friend, colleague, or family member before you try it live with real prospective customers. Set up a scenario and get them to role-play a typical prospective customer. Practice asking story-leading questions and guiding them through The Consequences Story. Before you know it, you'll be ready for the real thing.

As you practice and then move on to working with real customers, recognize that much of what you'll be doing here will be largely improvisational. You'll be dancing, taking cues from their words and their body language. You'll start to identify the music in their heads and it will guide you in the dance.

You'll be re-creating and viewing their story in your own mind and, as an intensely curious story listener, you'll want to discover where the next turn in the story leads them. So you'll ask a story-leading question, and then the next, and then the next after that.

There's an art to listening with great attention and letting their story steer you through an exploration of the future unfolding in their minds. It's a bit like being a tour guide—when you see a meaningful panorama or a significant vista, you pull over and let them explore it more closely through artful questions. Over time, you'll become more expert at spotting appropriate side roads to the main storyline, and at gracefully guiding them to powerful observation points.

You're a listener to their story, but not a passive listener. You play a key creative role in this process. In a sense, you'll be offering them threads as they spin their yarn and weave their tapestry. To a certain degree, your questions will guide the story, but only in harmony with their feedback and direction.

A good Consequences Story is truly a work of art!

Chapter Summary

- The Consequences Story is told by prospective customers as they imagine a future in which the worries and concerns they shared with you have become real. Your job is to be the catalyst for The Consequences Story by asking artful and thoughtful story-leading questions and then giving wonderful attention.

- The purpose of The Consequences Story is to help prospective customers see and experience the ramifications of not fixing their problems. It helps them avoid procrastination.

- Normally, you should help prospective customers develop a Consequences Story for each individual worry or concern they shared with you.

- The Consequences Story helps prospective customers take ownership of the ramifications of neglecting their problems.

- The Consequences Story must be their story, not yours. It doesn't count if you say it. It only counts if they say it.

- In some cases, the purpose of The Consequences Story can be achieved with the very lightest of touches.

- Imagining a scenario and narrating a story about what you are imagining can create the same sensations as experiencing a real event. As a result, in imagining and sharing The Consequences Story, prospective customers are able to see, speak, hear, and feel the consequences of their behavior. This combination of sensory input makes real the dangers of leaving their problems unaddressed.

- You can only make a sale when the perceived consequences of leaving the problem unaddressed, plus the perceived value of the benefits of fixing the problems outweigh the perceived cost of implementing the fix. The Consequences Story adds weight to the cost of leaving the problem uncorrected.

- Although this process may appear at first a bit contrived, experience has shown it won't seem that way to prospective customers, especially as you become more artful in forming your questions.

- It is essential to remember that no customer will go to a place beyond their comfort zone. If they create discomfort, it's because they themselves are willing to go there.

- Creating a Consequences Story with prospective customers is an improvisational dance that creates a beautiful work of art.

Chapter 12

The Benefits Story

Key Points

> The Benefits Story is the flip side of The Consequences Story. It is told by prospective customers as they imagine a future in which their worries and concerns have been properly addressed by your products and services.

> To create an effective Benefits Story, you must first provide a simple but credible assurance that you can answer their concerns and solve their problems.

> The Benefits Story must be their story, not yours. You guide it but they tell it. It doesn't count if you say it. It only counts if they say it.

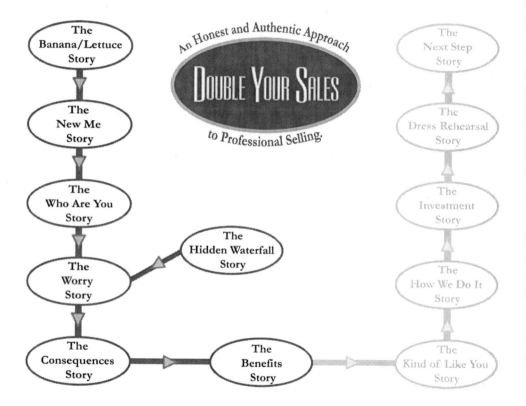

The Banana/Lettuce Story

The New Me Story

The Who Are You Story

The Worry Story

The Hidden Waterfall Story

The Consequences Story

The Benefits Story

An Honest and Authentic Approach

DOUBLE YOUR SALES

to Professional Selling.

The Next Step Story

The Dress Rehearsal Story

The Investment Story

The How We Do It Story

The Kind of Like You Story

What is The Benefits Story?

The Benefits Story is told by prospective customers about the potential impact of fixing the problems and concerns they have identified.

The Benefits Story is their narrative of a future in which their areas of concern have been handled. It is told in response to your story-leading questions, questions that invite them to look forward and picture what might occur if they find and implement answers to their problems.

What is the Purpose of The Benefits Story?

The purpose of The Benefits Story is to help prospective customers see and feel the impact of a decision to work with you and implement your answers and solutions to their problems. It helps them recognize and anticipate the positive results they can create for themselves and those they care about if they move forward.

The desire to avoid future pain is the most powerful human motivator. That is the theme of The Consequences Story, and that is why The Consequences Story comes first in the Double Your Sales process.

The second most powerful human motivator is a desire to create future happiness. If we are able to see that our behavior will make us and those we care about happier, we are likely to take action to strive for that happiness.

The Benefits Story gives prospective customers a preview of the happiness they can enjoy, and it motivates them to take steps to secure that happiness. It helps them see and feel the benefits of working with you and implementing your answers and solutions.

What is an Example of The Benefits Story?

In order to set the stage for The Benefits Story, you need to provide prospective customers a positive assurance that what you offer will address their concerns and solve their problems. Such an assurance might sound something like this:

> *Agent:* Bob, I think I now have a clear understanding of the dangers you and your family face if something were to happen to you before you could take action to address your lack of adequate life insurance. I have a process, which I will explain in a moment, that will allow us to determine the right amount of insurance for you, based on the needs of your family and the range of your budget. Through this process, we can make sure the consequences you've been describing won't happen to your family.

This statement of assurance is the fulcrum upon which the prospective customers' future story will pivot. It creates the mental shift from consequences to be avoided to benefits to be sought. Without this pivot, The Benefits Story does not have nearly as much credibility or impact.

After your assurance, you should outline a hypothetical future in which your products and services start to eliminate negative consequences and deliver positive benefits to these prospective customers and their loved ones.

As with The Consequences Story, The Benefits Story is told in response to your story-leading questions. Here is how it might sound:

> *Agent:* Bob, I'd like you to imagine that we decide to work together to create a life insurance plan that's just right for your family—not too large and not too small but just right for your needs and your budget. Then I'd like you to imagine that, tragically and unexpectedly, something happens to you. You're gone,

but now, instead of leaving your family in dire financial straits, because of life insurance, your family has sufficient money to deal with the worries we've been talking about. Compared to the scenario we imagined a minute ago, how might that change things for your wife as she has now become a single parent?

Bob: That's a much prettier picture. My wife would now have choices, positive choices. If she were to choose to stay at home with the children until they are older, she would have the money to do that. If she were to choose to go back to work, she would have the resources to hire the help she would need with the house and with the children.

Agent: How do you think that would affect her physical, mental, and emotional well-being?

Bob: That would be so much better for her. It would take so much stress and worry off her shoulders. It would relieve so many burdens.

Agent: And how would that affect the quality of care she would be able to give your children?

Bob: It would clearly help her be a much more patient and attentive parent. She's a very loving and caring mother; that's one reason I love her so much. With the financial resources behind her, she would be able to give them the care she feels for them in her heart.

Agent: That's a beautiful image you're describing. Bob, another of your concerns was about her difficulty in paying the mortgage on your house. If something were to happen to you and there were enough money for her to pay off the mortgage, how would that change things for your family?

Bob: That would make a huge difference for them. If they could stay in our house, and it were paid for, the good life we've been trying to create for ourselves and our children could go on. Of course there would be a lot of upheaval at my death, but the secondary disruptions of having to move out of the house could all be avoided. My wife could stay in a place she loves, and has spent so much time making beautiful. Our children could stay in a neighborhood they know already with all of their friends. Life for them could go on. It would be much easier for them to regain a sense of normalcy.

Agent: If they were to think about how you and your foresight had made all this possible for them, how do you think they would think about you?

Bob: I'm pretty sure they would feel grateful.

Agent: I'm certain they would. A third area of concern you mentioned was your children's education. If you can imagine we have built into your insurance plan sufficient resources to guarantee your children could go to the best colleges if they choose to, what would that look like?

Bob: I think if they knew they had the funds to attend any college they wanted, it would inspire them to work harder in school. The fact that I had provided those funds through proper insurance would hopefully help them understand education is a high priority for me and something I value deeply. Hopefully that will inspire them to set similar priorities for themselves.

Agent: And over the long haul, how would a world-class education help your children?

Bob: In my own life, I've seen that those who have a great education find many doors and opportunities open to them. With a great education, my children would be able to go as far as they chose to go. I'd like that for them.

Agent: Bob, you've mentioned a number of benefits that would come to you and your family with a proper life insurance plan. Are there any other benefits you can see that you haven't mentioned yet?

Bob: The thing that comes immediately to mind is I would be at peace, and so would my wife. We've been worried about this a lot, so once this is all taken care of, I think we'll be able to look at each other and say "We've done the best we can do for each other and our kids."

How Do You Use The Benefits Story?

Whereas The Consequences Story helps prospective customers focus on the damage that would result if they fail to address the dangers they've identified, The Benefits Story is the happy side. It's the story of the good things that can happen if those dangers and worries are eliminated.

The Benefits Story helps them recognize and appreciate the positive things that will come to them by working with you. It focuses their attention not on your products and services, but on the impact of those products and services in their lives. The Benefits Story makes it apparent they can create a better future for themselves and their loved ones by working with you.

As with The Consequences Story, you must remember The Benefits Story is their story, not yours. Once again, it doesn't count if you say it. It only counts if they say it. And they can't say it if they can't see it. Your job is to ask the kinds of questions that will allow them to imagine a future in which their worries and concerns have been properly addressed, and to describe the positive outcomes that will result.

What Are Some Tips For Using The Benefits Story?

As mentioned above, one important secret for using The Benefits Story is to provide a positive and credible assurance the products and services you offer and the process you use to select the appropriate products and services will deliver the results they need. At this stage of the meeting, they don't need to know *how* you will do that, but they do need to feel that you *can* do that.

As with The Consequences Story, the key to helping them narrate an effective Benefits Story is for you to recall the worries and concerns they identified earlier in The Worry Story. Keeping that list in mind, you should move systematically through their worries, asking them to picture and then tell you what it could look like if their concerns have been eliminated.

With each worry or concern, you should ask them to tell you what it will mean for them and those they care about to have that worry or concern out of the picture. Invite them to share that future perspective through the eyes of others as well as their own. Help them to envision both short-term and long-term outcomes. Help them to imagine and describe the secondary and tertiary benefits if they can.

I have found that after I work my way through each of the worries and the resulting benefits that will flow from handling those worries, it is nearly always effective to ask a broad, catchall story-leading question such as, "Besides the benefits we have already talked about, what others might result from our work together?"

Their answers to this "what more?" question will be truly amazing. They will identify benefits for themselves and their loved ones that would never have occurred to you. The length and breadth to which their minds will go with this "what more?" question are often far beyond anything you could imagine for them.

While The Benefits Story is often shorter than The Consequences Story, it does not need to be rushed. Allow prospective customers and yourself to relish the potential outcomes they will experience if their worries can be tackled.

There is an art to knowing when to draw The Benefits Story to a close. The key is to pay close attention to their tone of voice and to their body language and other nonverbal clues. When those tell you enough is enough, gently bring The Benefits Story to an end and start in to The Kind of Like You Story.

How Do You Create The Benefits Story?

The Benefits Story is usually much easier to create than The Consequences Story. That's because you're focusing on the positive and not the negative.

To create The Benefits Story, *you* need to be able to picture the positive outcomes that come to your customers as a result of using your products and services. It goes without saying you must authentically believe in what you are selling, and you must authentically believe what you offer is right and good for these prospective customers.

When you can comfortably picture the positive benefits that will come to them as they work with you, you simply need to ask them story-leading questions that allow them to picture those benefits in their own minds. It is important not to be too suggestive. Trust that with the right questions, prospective customers can see for themselves the benefits that will come to them.

Do not be concerned if the benefits they see and describe are not exactly the ones that come to your mind. What you are most concerned about is to make sure these are their projected benefits and this is their story. As with The Hidden Waterfall Story, where if it's not a worry for them, then it's not a worry for you, with The Benefits Story, if it's not a benefit for them, then it's not a benefit for you either.

As they tell The Benefits Story, your interest and your attention are essential to the quality of the thinking they will do and to the quality of the stories they will tell. It is essential that you not become so engrossed in thinking up your next question that you fail to listen carefully and generously to their answers.

How Do You Get Started Using The Benefits Story?

The best way to get started using The Benefits Story is to spend some time reflecting on the positive outcomes your products and services create for your customers. This will give you confidence in the value of what you offer, and this will in turn give you confidence as you invite prospective customers to consider the value of working with you.

Once again, role playing in a safe environment with colleagues, friends, or family will help you learn to ask graceful and elegant story-leading questions. Once again, you need to practice being a tour guide. That shouldn't be hard for The Benefits story, because on this tour, the views are all spectacular and the vistas are all beautiful.

Then it's time to jump in with real prospects. You'll soon discover The Benefits Story is easy.

Chapter Summary

- The Benefits Story is told by prospective customers as they imagine a future in which their worries and concerns have been properly addressed by using your products and services.

- Your job is to be the catalyst for The Benefits Story by asking artful and thoughtful story-leading questions and then listening and giving exceptional attention.

- The purpose of The Benefits Story is to help prospective customers see and experience the positive outcomes that will result from working with you and fixing their problems. It helps them envision, appreciate, and articulate the opportunities that will come to them from solving their problems.

- To create an effective Benefit Story, you must first provide a positive and credible assurance that you know how to deliver solutions to the prospective customers' problems.

- You should usually help prospective customers develop a Benefits Story that addresses each worry or concern they shared with you.

- The Benefits Story must be their story, not yours. It doesn't count if you say it. It only counts if they say it.

- The Benefits Story is usually easier and shorter than The Consequences Story. You must be sensitive and attentive so as not to drag it on too long.

- The quality of your listening and your attention will substantially affect prospective customers' ability to envision and describe the benefits of working with you.

Chapter 13

The Kind of Like You Story

Key Points

➤ The Kind of Like You Story describes a previous customer who had similar problems to these prospective customers, who used similar solutions to the ones you are proposing for them, and who enjoyed a happy outcome.

➤ The Kind of Like You Story is told sparsely and simply, inviting prospective customers to picture themselves in the story.

➤ The Kind of Like You Story reinforces the point that the way to avoid the ramifications identified in The Consequences Story and enjoy the positive results described in The Benefits Story is to use your products and services.

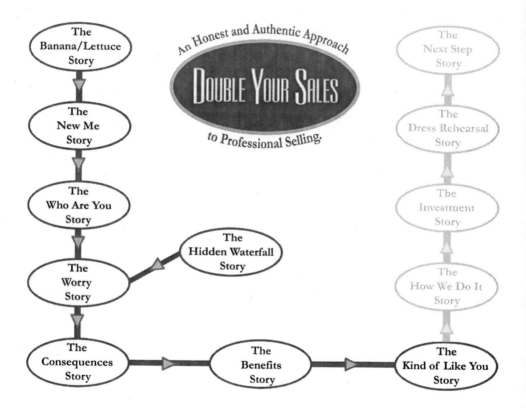

What is The Kind of Like You Story?

The Kind of Like You Story is a short, simple story that helps prospective customers picture themselves working with you, allowing them to enjoy the benefits and avoid the consequences they described earlier in The Consequences Story and The Benefits Story.

The Kind of Like You Story works because it allows prospective customers to envision themselves in the place of someone you helped in the past, someone with similar issues and concerns, someone with similar hopes and aspirations, and someone who used a similar solution to the one you're proposing.

Because of its simplicity and its sparse nature, The Kind of Like You Story invites prospective customers to complete the picture in their own mind by projecting themselves into the narrative. As a result, they are able to imagine themselves using your solutions to achieve a happy ending to their story.

What is the Purpose of The Kind of Like You Story?

The purpose of The Kind of Like You Story is to allow prospective customers to project themselves into a setting in which they are working with you and receiving the benefits of your process and your products and services. The Kind of Like You Story moves them to action because they see themselves in the picture, experiencing a happy ending by using your processes and your solution set, just like someone "kind of like" them.

The Kind of Like You Story invites them to create their own mental picture of the satisfaction they will feel when they become your customers. It helps them to see themselves avoiding the dangers and achieving the positive results they are seeking. The Kind of Like You

Story passively but powerfully invites them to imagine a different world in which their problems have been solved.

What Is an Example of The Kind of Like You Story Sound?

Here's an example of The Kind of Like You Story:

> You remind me a lot of a couple I worked with about a year ago. Like you, they were concerned about the safety of their investments in difficult financial times. They were about your age, they had a similar sized portfolio, and like you, they were originally from the Midwest. Unlike you, they were just moving to Florida.

> We showed them how our Wealth Builder & Protector Process could help them have a secure, comfortable, and active retirement. As a result of working together with our firm's process, they now have great confidence in achieving their financial goals. When I met with them last quarter, they were all smiles. They thanked me profusely for helping them achieve peace of mind about their financial situation.

How Do You Use The Kind of Like You Story?

You should use The Kind of Like You Story after you have identified the prospective customers' concerns in The Problem Story, helped them recognize dangers they may not have fully appreciated by using The Hidden Waterfall Story, invited them to imagine the future, where those problems have not been properly addressed using The Consequences Story, and allowed them to visualize the benefits that will come to them by addressing their worries through The Benefits Story.

The Kind of Like You Story should actually take only 30-60 seconds to tell. The Kind of Like You Story is successful because of its simplicity. The prospective customers hear you talk about someone similar to them, with similar concerns, hopes, and aspirations. They hear about someone who worked with you, using a similar solution or process as they will use with you. They hear you have helped create a successful outcome for those other customers.

The sparse details you share with them allow them to see themselves as the protagonists in the story. In other words, the story becomes a story about them, and in that story, because they are working with you, they achieve the satisfactory results they are seeking.

One of the keys to the effectiveness of this story is to provide the right amount of detail. It is important to give sufficient details about the other customers so these prospective customers can identify with them. Except for one point in which you make it clear they are not exactly like the earlier customers, each detail you provide needs to sound strikingly similar to the prospective customers in front of you.

Interestingly, it is also important not to provide too many details. Those extra details may start creating mental incongruities between these prospective customers and the previous ones. These disparities can interfere with their ability to see themselves in the story.

The Kind of Like You Story is based on a similar structure identified and described at length by Stephen Denning. In his book, *The Springboard*, Denning recognized that describing a fact pattern that was recognizable by his listeners and that invited them to project themselves into the story carried great force in moving his listeners to action.

The secret, Denning discovered, was to paint a word picture that was sufficiently familiar to his listeners that they could see themselves in it, but not so detailed and not so foreign that they had trouble projecting themselves into the story. This same structure occurs in The Kind of Like You Story.

What Are Some Tips For Using The Kind of Like You Story?

It is not necessary that the previous customers whose story you tell be exactly identical to these prospective customers. It only matters that the details you share about them be sufficiently similar to allow the prospective customers to project themselves into the narrative.

Once while I was working with a well-to-do gentleman in Mississippi who was considering the use of a charitable remainder trust to fund his vision for supporting teacher scholarships in the public schools in his home town, I used the example of Osceola McCarty as The Kind of Like You Story. My narrative sounded something like this:

> Mr. Smith, you remind me of a woman on the other side of the state, who was likewise very interested in public education in Mississippi. Her vision was to use her resources to help train teachers by offering scholarships at the University of Southern Mississippi. She established a charitable remainder arrangement to carry out her philanthropic objectives, which is the same planning tool I would recommend for you.

> I heard her speak recently about what she did, and I can tell you, she was beaming from ear to ear. She saw that her generous gift had made an enormous difference in the lives of teachers and for public education in the State of Mississippi.

In telling the story to my prospective customer, I focused on the similarities between his situation and Osceola McCarty's situation. I did not mention, however, that Osceola was black and had a net worth of approximately $200,000, whereas my prospective customer was white and had a net worth of several million dollars. Similarly, I did not point out that Osceola McCarty had grown up poor in Hattiesburg, Mississippi, whereas my customer had grown up in a family of privilege in the north and had migrated to Mississippi with his family's business. These details were irrelevant to the story I was telling him and to the point I was trying to make. They would have prevented my prospective customer from projecting himself into the story.

The net result of my story was my customer created a charitable remainder trust funded with substantial assets that benefited teachers in his community, consistent with my customer's larger mission to support public education in the State of Mississippi.

How Do You Create The Kind of Like You Story?

The creation of The Kind of Like You Story is very simple. It starts with the phrase, "You remind me of ...," and continues with a recitation of a few significant details about the prior customer that are similar to the prospective customers sitting with you. It continues with the statement "Unlike you, they..." and then points out one way in which those customers were different from these prospective customers.

It goes on to identify two or three issues that are similar in both cases. In addition, it includes a brief description of the process or solution you used (or your colleague used) in that prior case and which you intend to use with these prospective customers.

It concludes with a brief statement of the positive results that were achieved in that prior case. If possible, you should use the previous customers' own words (or a paraphrase) describing their experience and the results they enjoyed. A statement of a happy outcome is more convincing if it's in the words of the third party.

One of the secrets to being able to create and tell The Kind of Like You Story is to be able to recognize similarities and differences between the prospective customers sitting in front of you and customers from prior cases you have worked on or of which you are aware. The best place to find commonality is by focusing on The Worry Story.

Start with your list of 10 to 12 problems or issues you can effectively address. Then for each of those 10 to 12 areas of concern, identify three or four cases you or a colleague have handled in which that particular issue came up and was appropriately addressed.

Next, pick the one case out of the three or four that presents the most interesting story. Create a brief story based on that case for each of the 10 to 12 worry areas. Then practice each of the 10 to 12 stories, telling them quickly and sparsely, with only a minimal amount of detail.

When you meet with prospective customers, I recommend that you review your list of 10 or 12 issues you can address, and identify which ones are likely to be discussed in that meeting, based on your foreknowledge of the prospects and the meeting. Then review your list of possible Kind of Like You Stories that might apply to each of these 10 or 12 issues, and polish up on the ones you are likely to use.

How Do You Get Started Using The Kind of Like You Story?

It is important to practice these stories, and especially to practice being able to tell them simply in a sparse, unadorned manner. I recommend you practice with a watch, until you can tell them in no more than 30-60 seconds.

After you've finished the story, it is not necessary to solicit a customer reaction to it. Instead, segue immediately into The How We Do It Story.

Chapter summary

- The Kind of Like You Story is a simple, bare-bones narrative about someone "kind of like" these prospective customers who used your products or services in the past and achieved a satisfactory result.

- The Kind of Like You Story is told quickly, in approximately 30-60 seconds.

- The power of The Kind of Like You Story comes from its implicit invitation for prospective customers to envision themselves in the story, identifying with the problems and concerns of the person who is "kind of like" them, working through those problems by using your processes and solutions, and experiencing a happy outcome from doing so.

- In telling The Kind of Like You Story, it is important to identify similarities and avoid most discrepancies between the people in the story and the people to whom you are speaking..

- It is essential that The Kind of Like You Story have a happy ending. It is more powerful if the happy ending is expressed in the words or actions of a third party and not in your own words.

- At the end of The Kind of Like You Story, move quickly into The How We Do It Story.

Chapter 14

The How We Do It Story

Key Points

> The How We Do It Story is a narration of your process for delivering solutions to your customers.

> The How We Do It Story backs up your claims that you can fix these prospective customers' problems.

> You must have a process, especially if you sell products. Without a process and a How We Do It Story, your product will shortly become a commodity.

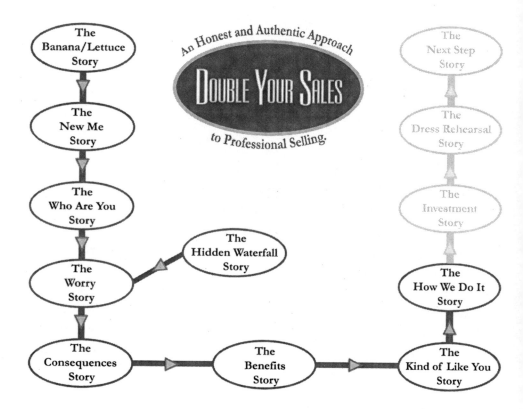

What is The How We Do It Story?

The How We Do It Story is a step-by-step narration of the process you use to address customers' worries and solve their problems. It is a story-based description of how you deliver your services or products.

What is the Purpose of The How We Do It Story?

The purpose of The How We Do It Story is to demonstrate to prospective customers that you have a system for finding the right answers to their problems and delivering solutions.

Several other purposes are achieved as you tell The How We Do It Story. The prospective customers see you are experienced, you understand people like them, and you know how to solve their problems. They see you are thoughtful and systematic. They see you will find appropriate solutions to their unique set of problems. They perceive added value in your approach because they have a clear understanding of how you work.

What is an Example of The How We Do It Story?

Here is an example of The How We Do It Story I use with prospective estate planning clients:

> Michael, we have designed a rather unique estate planning process we use when working with clients like you. I'd like to describe it to you, so that you'll have a clear picture of what it might look like if we choose to work together. I'm going to make a little sketch as I go along so you can visualize each step as I tell you about it.

The first step in our process is what we call "*The Get-Acquainted Conversation.*" That's the meeting we're having right now. The purpose of *The Get-Acquainted Conversation* is for us to get to know each other better, for me to understand the worries and concerns you have, for us to consider how I might help you address those concerns, and for both of us to decide whether it would make sense for us to go to the next step.

My approach to estate planning and financial planning is based on the principle that everyone has their own unique definition of the meaning of money, which has been created by them through a lifetime of experiences. I believe no one should work with an advisor who does not understand their unique definition of the meaning of money.

Before I take on a new customer, I need to determine whether they have a definition of money that will allow me to be the best advisor for them. In some cases, it's possible I would not be the best advisor to work with them, and I think we should find that out up front.

My many years of experience have taught me the best way to understand another person's unique definition of the meaning of money is to listen to their "meaning of money stories," which are the experiences that have defined money for them. To do that, I have created a tool kit that allows my clients to comfortably share several of their "meaning of money stories" with me in about 30 or 40 minutes. I call this "The Meaning of Money Priceless Conversation."

The Meaning of Money Priceless Conversation Tool Kit, which you see here, contains a booklet that explains why our "meaning of money stories" are so important to understanding how we see and feel about money. It also contains a set of questions that will help you recall and share with me some of the most significant meaning of money experiences in your life. These questions include things like,

- "How was money handled in your household when you grew up?"
- "What was your first job, what did you make from that job, and what did you learn about money from that experience?"
- "What was the best financial decision you've ever made?"
- "What was the worst financial decision you've ever made, and what did you learn from that mistake?"

So the next step in my process, as you can see in the diagram I'm making, is "*The Meaning of Money Conversation.*" In that meeting, I will interview you using the questions in this booklet and I will record that conversation using this small digital recorder. Three important things will come out of *The Meaning of Money Conversation.*

First, you will achieve greater clarity for yourself about what money means to you, and what you want money to do for you and for those you care about. Never before in your lifetime will you have had the opportunity to recall and share so many meaning of money stories at one time, with a person who is intensely interested in hearing your stories. By remembering them and talking about them, you will experience a much clearer sense of what you want to accomplish in planning for yourself, your loved ones, and your money.

The second thing that will happen is I, as your advisor, will have an authentic and unvarnished understanding of what money means to you, not filtered through some questionnaire or test booklet, but woven within the fabric of the stories of your life. This will help me become a much more effective advisor for you. This will help me create plans and propose options that will best suit you. By working together with you, and with the insight I will gain, we can create a plan that will make the biggest possible difference in your life and the lives of those you care about.

Third, the stories you tell will contain a lifetime of wisdom and insight about how to use money wisely. We will capture this wisdom and insight and save it on this audio CD in the kit. In the future, you may choose to share it with those people and causes you love who will be receiving your money sometime down the road. As a result, in the long run, they will receive not only your money, but your advice and your counsel and your life-learning about how to use money with greater skill and judgment. What could be more valuable than that?

By the end of *The Meaning of Money Conversation*, we will both have a realistic sense of whether it is right for us to work together, whether I should be your advisor and whether you should be my client.

If we both agree we should, then we will move to the next step, which I call "*The Design Session*," as you can see here in this diagram. In *The Design Session*, I will teach you about the law and you will teach me about yourself and your family and the things you most want to accomplish in our planning. Then, by putting our knowledge and insight together, we will jointly create the ideal estate plan for you and those you love. We will create a plan that addresses each one of the issues you have shared with me here today and many, many more which we have not yet discussed.

In *The Design Session,* you will see your hopes and dreams come alive, and you will see your worries and fears put to rest. The plan we create will be unique to you, and it will fit you and your situation like a custom-tailored suit.

After *The Design Session,* we will ask you to gather information about your assets and how they are owned or titled. This will allow us to make sure each thing you own is aligned correctly with your estate plan. While you're doing that, my team and I will be developing the documents and other pieces of your plan according to the design we have created together.

Within two weeks after *The Design Session,* we will meet in "*The Review & Signing Meeting.*" At that time, I will walk you through the documents we have created and show you how they accurately reflect the design itself. If you have any questions or concerns, we will discuss them until you are satisfied. Once you are pleased with everything, we will complete the signing and notarization process. We will make sure all the i's are dotted and all the t's are crossed.

With the asset information you have brought to us, we will start preparing for "*The Asset Integration Session.*" The purpose of that meeting is to make sure the title of all your assets is correctly aligned with the estate plan we have created, so the plan actually works the way we intend for it to. My team will also be putting together all the documents and your asset information in a stately binder that will keep it organized and make it easy for you to stay on top of your plan.

On an ongoing basis, we will invite you to join our "*Legacy Builder Program,*" which will allow us to keep your plan current and up to date and will facilitate the creation of your own personal Legacy Library. This will be a series of Priceless Conversations and other activities to make sure your life lessons and personal instructions to those you love are not lost.

As you can see, I have diagrammed all of this for you as we have been talking. I wonder if you have any questions about any step in our process?

How Do You Use The How We Do It Story?

In a sense, The How We Do It Story is The Banana/Lettuce Story for the next stage of your relationship. It establishes and clarifies expectations. It's a roadmap for the journey ahead, and thus it gives customers comfort and reassurance. They know where they are and where they are headed. They know they are in the hands of an experienced and confident guide.

A clear and powerful How We Do It Story speaks volumes about you and your company. It says you have been down this road many times before—so many times, in fact, you have created your own map for how to traverse this territory. You know all the twists and turns in the road, and you also know where the potholes are and how to avoid them.

A clear and powerful How We Do It Story says you have thought deeply about the kind of customer experience you want to create for them. You have put yourself in their shoes, and you understand what will be most helpful to them in addressing and solving their problems. You have seen the journey through their eyes.

A clear and powerful How We Do It Story says you are systematic and orderly. Because of your method, none of the pieces will fall through the cracks. Every piece will be handled smartly and expeditiously.

A clear and powerful How We Do It Story says you don't shoot from the hip, but you work carefully through a problem to find the best solutions. It says you don't glibly hand out quick answers, but you have an organized way to find the right answers. Today's astute consumers understand that because the world is changing so rapidly, today's clever answers will be wrong tomorrow. Instead of clever answers, you offer your customers a caring relationship and a thoughtful process for finding the right answers regardless of changes in the environment.

A clear and powerful How We Do It Story says it will be easy for you to create a customized solution for these prospective customers. Because much of the process is already thought through and laid out in advance, you will have plenty of time and attention to focus on the uniqueness of their situation.

A clear and powerful How We Do It Story says you will involve them in the process of finding the right answers for their problems. It says you believe in collaboration and teamwork. It says you believe *their thinking* is as vital to the process as your thinking. It says you value them, and the role they will play in solving their problems with you.

How Do You Create The How We Do It Story?

To create The How We Do It Story, you must first have a clear and understandable process. If you are primarily in a service business, the process you describe will be the steps you follow when you work with customers like those with whom you are speaking. Each step in your process, which represents a significant meeting or customer event, should have its own distinctive name. The process as a whole should be simple and easy to follow.

If your business is primarily selling products, it is even more imperative that you have a process and that you describe it by telling The

How We Do It Story. As the seller of products, you face a serious risk of becoming a commodity. A commodity is a product that is generic and is bought and sold strictly on price, like a bushel of wheat or a gallon of gasoline. Without a simple and understandable customer-service process, you will be perceived as a commodity and thus you will face serious pricing pressure as the only means to differentiate your products from others like them.

How, you may ask, can the seller of products talk about a process? The simplest way is to identify the steps you use to determine which products are appropriate for particular customers, and then add to that the steps you use to deliver your products to your customers and ensure that they are satisfied. If you have a successful business that sells products, you are probably already doing those things. All you have to do is to identify the steps you use and describe the entire sequence in the form of a story—The How We Do It Story. Just as sellers of services, each step of your process should have its own unique name and the process as a whole should be simple and easy to understand.

In telling The How We Do It Story, as you name and describe each step, you should describe what happens in that step and what its purposes are. Your description should allow prospective customers to visualize that step as it will happen, thus making each step real and meaningful to their experience. If important actions take place before or after any of the meetings, or if customers will have assignments to complete to get ready for any of the steps, you should describe those activities as part of your story.

For purposes of telling the story, I recommend your process consist of no fewer than three steps and no more than seven steps. If you have a well-defined process that has more than seven steps, I recommend you pare down the number for purposes of telling The How We Do It Story.

Please note: I am *not* saying to change the underlying process. I am only suggesting that *in telling the story*, you group some steps together or simplify the end of the process by combining several steps into a single step, which will be unbundled later as you arrive at that stage in your relationship.

In this first meeting, it is not necessary to describe your entire life-long relationship process. It is important that prospective customers come away with the sense that your process is clear and understandable and manageable. Describing it with too many steps may make it seem overwhelming.

Another key ingredient to a successful How We Do It Story is to draw a simple "boxes-and-arrows" diagram of the process as you tell the story. This is done by making and labeling a box for each step in your process and then joining that step with the next one with an arrow. This rudimentary picture will reinforce the story you are telling and not distract from it.

At the end of your meeting, you should give the diagram to the prospective customers. In my experience, they will hold onto it and follow it throughout the process of working with you, using it as a roadmap to keep their bearings as they move through the project.

Sometimes when I teach this idea of a simple, hand-drawn diagram to salespeople, they show me beautiful graphic designs of their customer process, and they contend their professionally designed and multicolor printed process will be more compelling to prospective customers as they tell The How We Do It Story. I disagree. I believe that a formal flowchart or diagram will cause prospective customers to "go analytical."

Human nature is such that, the minute you put an elaborate schematic drawing in front of someone, they will immediately begin to analyze it and try to understand it. They will stop listening to your story and start focusing on the diagram. This will automatically switch them to the left side of the brain at precisely the wrong moment in the sales process. The last thing you want them to do, just before they make a decision whether to purchase your products or services, is to stop listening to you and get over in the left side of their brains.

By contrast, a simple, hand-drawn diagram that you create as you tell the story will reinforce your narration, will maintain the prospective customers' attention on you, and will keep their thinking on the right side of the brain. It will also reinforce the perception that your services or products will be uniquely and appropriately tailored to them and their problems.

If you have a beautiful graphic image of your process, you may want to give it to them at the end of the meeting, but you should not use it while you are telling the story. As they are leaving and after they say yes to buying from you, you might hand it to them and say something like, "Here is how our graphic designer interpreted the process we use for clients like you, the one I told you about earlier. If you'd like to use this instead of the one I made by hand, you're welcome to have it."

What Are Some Tips For Using The How We Do It Story?

I have learned that as you describe your process to prospective customers, it is important that you point out how your process will answer their specific problems and concerns. Even the world's most brilliant process is useless if it doesn't fix the problems at hand. As you tell The How We Do It Story, it must be clear where in the process you will address their worries. It is also helpful to mention there are many other worries you have not yet discussed that will be solved in the course of following your process.

It has been my experience that describing your unique and thought-ful process in a narrative fashion will do more to enhance the value of your products or services than just about anything you can do. Having a clearly defined methodology to solve your customer's problems gives you and them confidence that working together will be mutually beneficial.

One of the reasons this is true is because, as you describe your unique process, you are able to elaborate on the specifics of how you solve your customers' problems, and you get to point out how the way you address their problems it is different from your competition's approach.

I find it interesting to note that if you were simply to say, "We can do this and this and this and this for you," it would sound like brag-ging. In the context of telling them the story of your process, however, it doesn't come across that way at all. The story format softens your descriptions and explanations for how you solve your customers' prob-lems and makes you more credible.

In a sense, The How We Do It Story closes the circle on the claims you made earlier in the meeting. Before, you said, in essence, "You're here because you have problems. I understand those problems. I even recog-nize dangers you may not be aware of. I can see, along with you, that serious consequences will occur if your problems are not properly addressed. I can see there are incredible benefits to be enjoyed if your problems can be resolved. In the past I have helped other people similar to you solve problems similar to yours. Now, here's how we do it; here's how together we will solve your problems." Now the circle is complete.

How Do You Get Started Using The How We Do It Story?

To get started, you must first get clear about your process. You should create your own boxes-and-arrows diagram with no less than three steps and no more than seven. Each step should have its own distinctive name.

With your diagram in hand, try telling The How We Do It Story to a safe and willing listener. Practice describing each step and explaining the purpose of each step from the perspective of a potential customer. Imagine they have identified three of the 10-12 problems that you can fix; in your story, point out where in your process each problem area will be addressed. Ask your listener to give you honest feedback.

Once you're comfortable telling the story with a pre-drawn diagram, try it again starting with a blank sheet of paper, so you can practice making the sketch as you tell the story.

When you're at ease with that, you're ready to try it with real prospective customers. You'll soon discover that telling The How We Do It Story is easy, fun, and very powerful

Chapter Summary

- The How We Do It Story is a story-based, step-by-step description of how you determine which products or services are right for these customers, how you deliver those products or services, and how they solve the customers' problems.

- The purpose of The How We Do It Story is to demonstrate intuitively you have a system for finding the right answers to their problems and delivering solutions.

- In addition, The How We Do It Story shows you are experienced, understanding, thoughtful, systematic, solution-oriented, flexible, collaborative, and valuable to your customers.

- The How We Do It Story establishes and clarifies expectations for the next stage of your relationship with these prospective customers.

- It is absolutely essential that you start with a clear and understandable process.

- For purposes of telling The How We Do It Story, the process you describe should consist of between three and seven steps.

- If you sell products, you must have a unique process; otherwise you are in danger of becoming a commodity, sold only on the basis of the lowest price.

- If you sell products, your How We Do It Story should describe how you help customers identify accurately what they need and how you deliver your products to ensure customer satisfaction.

- Each step of your process must have a customer-friendly name.

- You should sketch your process by hand using a simple boxes-and-arrow diagram, as you tell The How We Do It Story. Do not use a printed or computer-generated graphic image, as this will cause prospective customers to "go analytical" on you and not listen to your story.

- It is critical during The How We Do It Story that you point out how your process solves the worries they identified earlier in the meeting.

- The How We Do It Story is one of the most powerful value-enhancers you can use in a sales meeting, because it closes the circle of the claims and assertions you made earlier in the meeting.

Chapter 15

The Investment Story

Key Points

> A good Investment Story helps prospective customers connect the cost of your goods and services to something they understand from their experience. It gives personal meaning to the dollar number.

> The key question in developing your Investment Story is "How can I present pricing information to prospective customers so they have a context for weighing value versus cost?"

> A good Investment Story creates personal relevance for the investment that prospective customers are about to make with you. It helps them see that investment within the larger canvas of who they are and their worries and concerns. It creates a context within which information about the cost of your goods or services can resonate both intuitively and analytically with them.

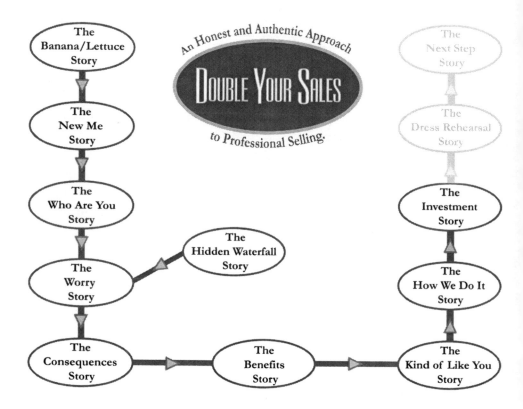

The Banana/Lettuce Story → The New Me Story → The Who Are You Story → The Worry Story ← The Hidden Waterfall Story

The Worry Story → The Consequences Story → The Benefits Story → The Kind of Like You Story → The How We Do It Story → The Investment Story → The Dress Rehearsal Story → The Next Step Story

An Honest and Authentic Approach

DOUBLE YOUR SALES

to Professional Selling.

What is The Investment Story?

The Investment Story is a narrative describing what and how prospective customers pay for the goods and services you offer. There is always something more to talk about than just "the number." The Investment Story is that "something more."

What is the Purpose of The Investment Story?

Before prospective customers can make a buy or no-buy decision, they must know what your goods or services cost, as well as when and how they will pay for them. But you must be smart about how you deliver that information. Raw numbers are purely analytical and, standing alone, are difficult for even the left brain to process, especially in a sales meeting.

The purpose of The Investment Story is to help prospective customers connect the cost of your goods and services to something they understand from their experience. It gives personal meaning to the dollar figure.

The Investment Story creates a context within which price information will resonate both intuitively and analytically with your prospective customers, thus allowing them to weigh cost versus value, and leading them more readily to a decision to say "yes."

What is an Example of The Investment Story?

There is a wide spectrum of goods and services available for purchase, and in the ways customers pay for them. On one end of the spectrum, the item for purchase is tangible and well-understood and the price is well known to the buying public. On the other end, the potential purchase is intangible and unknown or mysterious to the buying public, and its price is likewise unknown or mysterious. In between, there are millions of variations.

Because of this diversity, it is impossible to present a single example of The Investment Story that covers all the possibilities. Presenting concrete products to prospective customers creates different challenges from presenting intangible services. Well-publicized prices may be harder or easier to discuss than unknown prices, depending on the circumstances. As a result, creating your own Investment Story may require an added measure of creativity and imagination from you. There is not a one-size-fits-all formula here.

That said, there are some common principles that apply in most situations. I like the following real-life example used by "Greg," an estate planner in a large city in the Midwest, because of its brilliant way of using a story to create a context for discussing with prospective customers the substantial fees he charges for his very intangible services.

In presenting this example, I am not suggesting it is the model you should follow. Greg's Investment Story fits his personality and works in his environment, but it probably wouldn't work for a lot of people. What I want you to notice is how his Investment Story works for him and how it creates a context within which the information about the cost of his services resonates with prospective customers both intuitively and analytically.

> *Greg:* Now that I've told you how our process will address the potential disasters you're trying to avoid, we need to talk about how much you'd need to invest to create a plan to accomplish your objectives.

> To help you understand that investment, I want to tell you about something that happened to me not long ago. My wife and I have been fussing for years about the quality of our conversations.

I've been telling her that she mumbles and she's been telling me that I'm deaf. She finally got tired of the fussing and dragged me down to the audiologist. Turns out she was right and I was wrong.

He did a lot of tests and found out that I have nearly 80% hearing loss in my left ear, as well as some loss in my right ear. As my wife can confirm, that's enough to create a lot of issues when you're around people. Even though I didn't even know beforehand that there was anything wrong, once I became aware of the problem and he showed me what a difference it would make to take care of it, it was clear I had to take action.

The audiologist laid out my options for me. One possibility, he said, was to do nothing. If I chose that option, my hearing and my relationship with my wife, family, clients, and others would continue to get worse. While the *apparent* cost of that approach would be zero, the *actual* long-term costs would be much higher.

A second option, he said, was to use a less expensive variety of hearing aid costing about $750. Such a hearing aid would sit on the back of my ear and it wouldn't have the same sound quality. He said from his experience, he could not recommend the $750 behind-the-ear hearing aid.

He said it would not only affect the quality of what I was hearing, it would also affect the way I thought about myself and the way other people related to me. "You'll feel 'different' with this on your ear, and other people will treat you as though you were 'different.'"

When I tried it out, the sound quality was better than without it, but it still wasn't perfectly clear. And I was definitely self-conscious of having that thing stuck on the back of my ear.

"What other choices do I have?" I asked him.

He then fitted me with a very tiny state-of-the-art hearing aid that fit completely inside my ear and was almost invisible. He said, "This is not going to be inexpensive but it will fully address your problem. You'll be able to hear. You'll be able to understand your wife, your clients in client meetings, and other people in other settings.

"Because of its size, most people won't even notice it unless you call it to their attention, and they won't treat you like you're handicapped or something. Soon, it will feel totally natural and comfortable to you."

He was right. The sound quality was remarkable. I could even hear my wife and she wasn't mumbling.

"So what's it cost?" I asked.

"Four thousand dollars," he said, "and I think you'll find it's worth every penny."

Greg then takes the tiny hearing aid out of his ear and shows it to the prospective clients. They're always impressed with how tiny it is.

> Greg: I paid $4,000 for this little piece of plastic, and it has changed my life. I can hear my wife, I can hear my clients, and most importantly, I can hear my one-year-old granddaughter. And to think that I didn't even know I had a problem, much less a $4,000 problem, when I came to see him. But it turned out to be one of the best investments I ever made.

Now let me tell you why I told you about my hearing aid. As it turns out, the average investment for base planning for clients like you with the serious estate planning issues you have is around that same $4,000 figure.

Remember the three areas of concern you shared with me: preserving privacy and control for your family; reducing taxes at both the state and federal level; and protecting the money being left to children and grandchildren from divorces, predatory lawsuits, and poor investment decisions? Those are serious challenges that our planning process can address, as well as other issues we haven't even talked about yet.

Right now you may be thinking the same thing I was thinking when I was at the audiologist's: "Four thousand dollars for that little tiny piece of plastic?" And I didn't even know I had a problem.

For a little piece of plastic, I paid $4,000 and I found that it's been worth every penny. Now, the work you're going to do with me, if you choose to work with me, will not be inexpensive, because we only do high quality work in this office.

There are cheaper ways to do this. You could go to a document preparation service or even to the internet and pull off documents if that's all you're looking for. However, my many years of experience have showed me that cheaper almost always ends up costing more in the long run, both financially and in the number of problems it creates for you and your loved ones when you get sick, have a stroke, or die. Our process is what you need to properly take care of your situation.

For your convenience, we break that fee down into three equal payments, one when you retain us, one when we complete the design, and one when we sign the final documents. We can take payments in cash, by check, or even credit card if you prefer. We'll work with you to make it as easy as possible.

How Do You Use The Investment Story?

The point of the example of Greg's story is not that we need to compare our fees and services to hearing aids, but to recognize how his Investment Story creates a context for the number that he puts on the table. Because of that story, prospective customers have something they can understand and relate to, something that gives meaning to the number itself. Thus the narrative creates context for prospective customers.

Notice that Greg refers to the cost of his services as an "investment." For some prospective customers, this language conveys that there's a potential return on the investment, it can pay future dividends, and it's not strictly an expense.

Notice also that in addition to talking about the cost itself, Greg also talks about the payment process. He mentions partial payments, timing of payments within his process, financing options, and methods of payment, such as check or credit card. This creates more of a "narrative flow" to the price discussion.

Finally, notice how Greg uses one story to tell another story. His Investment Story, which tells prospective customers that his fee will be about $4,000, uses the story of his trip to the audiologist to communicate several important points about his fees and the benefits of working with him.

Those points include the need to resist the temptation to do nothing, the real costs of inferior quality, the relational benefits of addressing what appear to be non-relational problems, and the fact that sometimes we have major problems we may not even recognize. This "story-within-a-story" technique can often be very effective, especially in situations like this when prospective customers are very likely to "go analytical" on you.

How Do You Create The Investment Story?

The first step to creating your Investment Story is to review what you're doing already. You may not need to change much if what you're doing works, especially if you have a simple pricing model, concrete products, and well-publicized prices. In that case, you should think through your pricing and payment process carefully and become more familiar and comfortable with the logistics of pricing and payment. Then determine how you can weave that information naturally into your Investment Story narrative.

On the other hand, if you don't have a simple pricing model, concrete products, and well-publicized prices, or if what you are currently doing isn't working as well as you would like, you will need to make further changes to your Investment Story, beyond weaving pricing and payment information into your narrative.

The key question in revamping your Investment Story is "How do I present pricing information to prospective customers so they can have a context for weighing value versus cost?" Here are four pointers to consider as you create your own unique Investment Story.

First, you need to present information about price in the form of a narrative. Story-based information is more easily understood and less likely to be criticized and rejected. Even if it's not a full-blown story with a plot, a hero, and a cast of characters, you have to describe in narrative fashion the cost of whatever you're selling and the way customers pay for it.

That narrative may sound something like, "first we do this, and then second you do that, and then, if you like, we do such-and-such, which is going to cost about x dollars, and here are some options as to terms and financing, etc."

Second, find something comparable, or something your prospective customers can understand and relate to, in order to create a context for the numbers. These "comparables" may be as literal and direct as a realtor's use of sales of similar houses of similar square footage, bedrooms, and bathrooms in the same or nearby neighborhoods, or as diverse as hearing aids and estate planning. The common denominator is that the items being compared to your products or services are understandable to your prospective customers.

Imagination and creativity are helpful in finding good comparables for your Investment Story. It also helps to be able to put yourself in the shoes of prospective customers. Not too long ago I was discussing estate planning fees with a residential housing developer and builder. I wanted him to understand that I could give him a range, but I wouldn't know precisely what my services would cost until we finished the "Design Session," at which time I would give him an exact quote.

Sensing that he was still a little uncomfortable with my approach, I asked him how he would answer if I came to his business and asked him to tell me how much he would charge to build me a new custom home.

"Well, that would depend on a number of factors," he said.

"Like what?" I asked.

"Like how many square feet would be in the house, the subdivision and lot where the house would be built, how fancy or plain you wanted the construction, the floor plan, how many extras and amenities, how much . . ."

His voice trailed off, and then he grinned at me. "Oh, I get it. Doing an estate plan the way you do it is like the way I build custom homes for my customers—I can't tell them what the cost will be until I know what they want me to build for them. I can give them ranges and approximate costs per square foot, but the final cost depends on what they need and want in a home."

"Exactly!" I said. "As I said a minute ago, I'll charge you $375 to conduct the 'Meaning of Money Conversation' because we can both see what that involves and the stand-alone value that experience will create for you. But you won't owe me anything for the estate planning until we design your plan together and we both know what I am going to create for you. Then I'll tell you my fees for that and you can decide then whether to go forward. Does that sound fair?"

"Totally fair," he replied.

A third pointer is, as you tell The Investment Story, to continue to refer to the prospective customers' earlier stories, including The Who Are You Story, The Worry Story, The Consequences Story, and The Benefit Story. In other words, nest the story of the investment they're about to make within the larger context of who they are, why they're there meeting with you, and what are their concerns, hopes, dreams, and fears for the future. Create personal relevance for the investment they are about to make. Help them see the connection between who they are, what worries they have, and what they are buying from you.

Finally, use humor if possible. There is likely to be a certain amount of tension as you get close to "the big reveal" on price, so lighten up if at all possible. Notice in Greg's story above how he uses humor effectively to soften the mood, by talking about the banter between himself and his wife, and joking about his hearing loss. Tasteful humor is always a good strategy in situations like these.

What Are Some Tips For Using The Investment Story?

Here are a couple of ideas to keep in mind. First, don't make your Investment Story unnecessarily complicated. Obviously, the whole concept of telling The Investment Story indicates that too simple (as in "The cost is x dollars, do you want it or not?") is not desirable. But it is possible to go too far in the other direction, putting too many variables and contingencies on the table.

Having options with regard to simple things such as methods of payment and financing is good, because it avoids putting prospective customers in a take-it-or-leave-it corner, and no one wants to feel they've been backed into a corner. But overly complex options can create confusion and a tendency to just say no. The nearly-universal knee-jerk response to confusion is to stay put and stand pat.

Complex options also draw Mr. Analytical out at precisely the time when you need most to be addressing Mr. Intuitive. You should carefully consider whether the buying options you are putting on the table are simple and understandable, or complex and confusing. Complex and confusing usually equal "no," or at least "not now."

A second idea to consider in the case of big-ticket sales is to offer a smaller, incremental purchase that allows prospective customers to take a small but significant step toward the big purchase, rather than asking for the whole thing at once. A smaller, incremental purchase encourages the relationship to develop further in the direction of the ultimate purchase.

I've found it's much easier to initially sell a small part of the project, like a Meaning of Money Conversation, than a $10,000 estate plan. So long as the prospective customers perceive real value in the small project, and so long as the small project leads us almost inexorably toward the main event (which in my case has always been true), then this is a good strategy. It should not be used, however, merely to procrastinate putting the buying issue on the table or if it doesn't ultimately result in the larger sale.

How Do You Get Started Using The Investment Story?

As you revamp your Investment Story, you'll definitely want to practice telling it in a safe environment before you go "live" with prospective customers. Of all the stories in the Double Your Sales process, this is the one that needs to sound the most natural and confident to prospective customers. Unfortunately, it is the one that is most likely to make you feel uncomfortable, because at this stage of the sales meeting, things are getting pretty serious and they're about to make a buying decision.

You can combat nervousness in the Investment Story through lots of practice, coupled with quality feedback. With this story, it is very helpful to get input from several different colleagues, friends, or family members, and then follow that up with more practice.

There's no shortcut here. You need to invest sufficient time and energy to polish your Investment Story and make it the best it can be.

Chapter Summary

- The Investment Story is a narrative describing what and how prospective customers pay to receive the goods or services you offer. There is always something more to talk about than just "the number." The Investment Story is the story of that "something more."

- The purpose of The Investment Story is to create a context within which information about the cost of your goods or services and how and when they pay will resonate both intuitively and analytically. This increases the likelihood prospective customers will say yes.

- A good Investment Story for you should fit you and your style, and should create a context within which the information about the cost of your goods or services connects with your prospective customers.

- A good Investment Story helps prospective customers understand the cost of your goods and services by connecting something from their experience with what you sell. It gives additional meaning to the number itself. The narrative creates context for prospective customers.

- The Investment Story must be told in the form of a narrative.

- A good Investment Story refers to the cost of your goods and services as an "investment." It also includes details of the payment process.

- You should nest the story of your prospective customers' investment within the larger context of who they are, why they're meeting with you, and what are their concerns, hopes, dreams, and fears for the future. You should seek to create personal relevance for the investment they are about to make.

- Use tasteful humor to lighten the mood.

- Complexity and confusion in pricing options usually cause analysis paralysis. Keep your pricing options and your Investment Story simple and understandable.

- In the case of big-ticket sales, consider offering a smaller, incremental purchase that moves prospective customers toward the larger purchase, rather than asking for the whole thing up front.

Chapter 16

The Dress Rehearsal Story

Key Points

➤ The purpose of The Dress Rehearsal Story is to intentionally turn the sales meeting "analytical," and thus bring Mr. Analytical squarely into the conversation, giving you the opportunity to influence your prospective customers' left-brain thinking.

➤ There are at least a dozen variations of The Dress Rehearsal Story. To decide which version of The Dress Rehearsal Story to use in a particular situation, ask yourself "What feels comfortable to me?" and "What will get these prospective customers to examine their decision from the analytical side of the brain?"

➤ Besides solidifying the buying decision and addressing concerns, the Dress Rehearsal Story is also a good time to check on how well you communicated during the meeting.

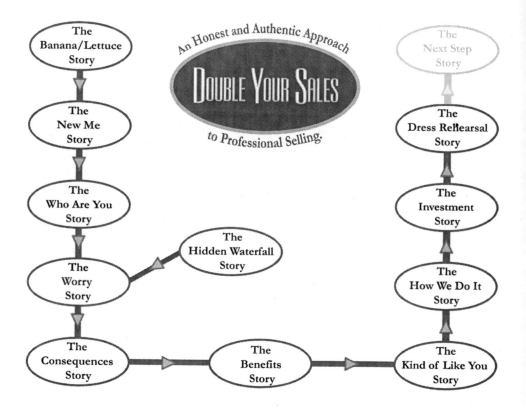

The Banana/Lettuce Story

The New Me Story

The Who Are You Story

The Worry Story

The Hidden Waterfall Story

The Consequences Story

The Benefits Story

An Honest and Authentic Approach

DOUBLE YOUR SALES

to Professional Selling.

The Next Step Story

The Dress Rehearsal Story

The Investment Story

The How We Do It Story

The Kind of Like You Story

What is The Dress Rehearsal Story?

The Dress Rehearsal Story is a technique for intentionally turning the meeting "analytical" and speaking to the left side of prospective customers' brains. It can take any number of forms, all with the objective of bringing Mr. Analytical squarely into the conversation during the meeting, thus giving you an opportunity to influence his thinking.

What is the Purpose of The Dress Rehearsal Story?

The sequence and flow of the Double Your Sales process is based on our human tendency to make significant decisions intuitively first and then to justify them analytically. We go with our gut, and then we turn to our head. Mr. Intuitive gets us moving and then Mr. Analytical jumps in to make sure we don't hurt ourselves.

At the beginning of a Double Your Sales meeting, you meet prospective customers where they are, usually on the analytical side. You invite them to the right side by using right-brain oriented approaches, primarily stories. You present your case for why they should buy from you. They decide. If the answer is "yes" or even "maybe," you turn the meeting hard to the left to engage Mr. Analytical on your terms so he will feel involved in the decision and so he will not seek to unravel the decision after the meeting.

The purpose of The Dress Rehearsal Story is just that—to turn the meeting analytical, thus drawing prospective customers' left brains into the decision-making process before they leave the meeting. This serves to engage both sides of their brains in the buying decision and to inoculate them from the dreaded "buyer's remorse:" changing their minds after they leave.

Let's step back and look at the big picture so far.

At the beginning of a sales meeting, prospective customers are nearly always guarded and critical—clearly in their left brain. You must meet them there and then invite them over to the right side of their brains in order to make a sale.

You start with The Banana/Lettuce Story, which initially speaks to the serial, orderly, and protective Mr. Analytical inside your prospective customers' heads. By meeting him front and center, you honor him and partially defuse his anxiety. Having done his duty by guiding and guarding the agenda of the meeting, Mr. Analytical is able to relax and allow Mr. Intuitive to step into the picture.

You then speak to Mr. Intuitive, using the language of story he understands so well. Your New Me Story and your prospective customers' Who Are You Story move the meeting to the right side of the brain.

At that point, your objective is to hold the meeting there as you guide your prospective customers to explore and articulate their worries, the consequences of not addressing their worries, and the benefits of finding solutions to their worries. The Worry Story, The Hidden Waterfall Story, The Consequences Story, and The Benefits Story use narrative to achieve that objective.

You continue to use stories to share an example of a previous customer kind of like them, to outline the process you will use to help them fix their problems, and to describe the investment required to purchase your solutions to their problems. These are the roles of The Kind of Like You Story, The How We Do It Story, and The Investment Story.

At the end of The Investment Story, you should ask them to buy from you. You must ask for the business.

Your aim is to make sure that at the moment at which you ask them to make a buying decision, they are primarily in their right brain where buying decisions originate. Hopefully, they say "yes" to your invitation, or at least "maybe" or "we're thinking about it."

If they do, you initiate an analytical discussion that engages their left brain. Your aim is to preempt Mr. Analytical's anticipated assault on Mr. Intuitive and his decision to buy. Rest assured that Mr. Analytical will question the decision sooner or later. You want that to happen sooner, while Mr. Intuitive is still energized from what's gone on already in the sales meeting and while you're there, so you can participate in the conversation.

What you don't want to happen is for Mr. Analytical to leave the meeting feeling that he hasn't been consulted, that Mr. Intuitive has gone off on his own (yet again!) and decided to buy something without involving Mr. Analytical in the process. When that happens, you can expect Mr. Analytical to pick a quarrel with his brain-mate. And in that tussle, Mr. Analytical, being the more forceful of the two, usually wins. If that happens, prospective customers end up resenting their decision to buy, or they back out altogether and you end up experiencing the dreaded "buyer's remorse."

Another danger is that prospective customers may get into a conversation with another person in which that other person asks questions requiring analytical answers. If their decision was purely intuitive and their left brain wasn't sufficiently engaged in the process, they may be unprepared to answer tough questions. If that happens, prospective customers may end up doubting their decision and themselves, and mistrusting you. Once again, this may cause them to back out of the deal.

The purpose of The Dress Rehearsal Dialogue is to head off those disasters.

What is an Example of The Dress Rehearsal Story?

The Dress Rehearsal Story takes its name from an experience I had in Philadelphia a few years ago. I was hired to teach the sales team of a company that offered a wonderful product for seniors—the opportunity to stay in their own homes for the rest of their lives.

One of the greatest worries of many senior citizens is that they will lose their ability to live independently and be forced to go to a nursing home, or to move in with one of their children and become a burden to them. This Philadelphia company offered an underwritten program that managed all the services necessary for seniors to stay in their own homes, from the moment they lost the ability to manage their own affairs, through their disability and on until their death. The company assumed responsibility for organizing and overseeing medical care, nursing care, meals, cleaning, plumbing, painting, yard care, everything seniors needed to live in their own homes. It was, literally, a dream come true for an older person to discover that this possibility was available.

When they called me and told me about their product, I was very impressed. I assumed that a product that was a dream come true for virtually every senior I had ever met would be selling like hot cakes. I was very surprised and perplexed to learn they weren't closing many sales. That's why they called me.

The program was expensive, but that wasn't the problem. The salespeople were seeing plenty of qualified prospective customers in the high-end market. The people they were contacting could easily afford this product.

The company was associated with a well-respected religious group, so they had excellent credibility and trust with prospective customers. The salespeople were cordial, knowledgeable, and articulate. They seemed to be doing everything right, but one thing was wrong: they couldn't land customers.

In working with them, I made a very interesting discovery. The salespeople reported that their initial meetings with prospective customers were almost always wonderful. The prospects were extremely pleased and excited to learn that their fondest dream could come true—they could stay in their own home and "Life Care at Home" would take care of just about everything for them. They were not balking at the price—after all, the value provided was extraordinary and the cost was well within the means of the prospective customers. They were warm and hospitable to the salesperson. They also loved that a trusted religious organization was behind the program.

Multiple meetings were needed to close a sale because the price of the product was based in part on the prospect's health. At the end of the first meeting, the medical exams were arranged and the second meeting was scheduled. Everyone was all smiles and looking forward to working together. Mentally, the salespeople were already cashing their commission checks.

The problem showed up at the second meeting. Curiously, between the first and second meetings, the excited and appreciative Dr. Jekyll somehow became an upset and accusatory and sometimes vicious Mr. Hyde. Kind and mild little old ladies turned into Tasmanian devils. Not only were they not ready to buy, they were ready to boot the salespeople out the door.

The salespeople were completely baffled by this about-face. They could occasionally recover the prospects' good will and make a sell, but not very often. Usually the second meeting was the last.

As I unraveled this mystery, it turned out that between the first meeting and the second, these prospective customers were talking with someone else about their "wonderful discovery," someone else who didn't necessarily share their deep fear of going to a nursing home or moving in with children, and someone who was often aghast at the price tag. This "someone else" was often an out-of-state child who was sure they could take care of mom or dad when the time came, or it was the prospect's CPA or financial advisor, whom the prospect approached about where to get the $20,000 to $30,000 down payment for the program.

These caring and well-intended children or advisors of course had legitimate questions about the details and the reliability of the program. They were naturally concerned that someone might be trying to take advantage of a vulnerable senior citizen.

The more questions they asked and the more concerns they raised, the more confused and troubled the seniors became. Unable to find adequate responses to these questions and concerns, the prospective customers started to question themselves and to doubt the salespeople. Questioning and doubting quickly turned into suspicion and anger toward the salespeople. When the salespeople returned, they ran into this wall of hostility.

An awareness of left brain/right brain behavior in sales settings helped me recognize what was happening. In the initial meeting, the prospective customers got caught up in the euphoria of discovering the perfect answer to one of their gravest fears. The salespeople, sensing an easy sale, added to the feel-good mood, and everyone was swept along in a wave of positive emotion. The prospects' decisions to buy were purely intuitive, untempered by any input from the analytical side of the brain.

Unfortunately, when the emotions waned and especially in the stark light of challenging questions from someone else, the prospective customers were unprepared to explain their excitement *analytically*. Sure, they could share how wonderful they felt about it *intuitively*, but they had no left-brain answers and were left feeling stupid. When we feel stupid, we pull back, clam up, get angry, and look for someone to blame. The salespersons became the logical targets of that blame and anger.

Once I diagnosed the problem and explained to the sales team what was happening, it all started to make sense to them. With the proper diagnosis, implementing an effective remedy was relatively simple. The solution was to walk through a "dress rehearsal" of the anticipated conversation prospective customers would be having with their child, advisor, or someone else they identified. It sounded something like this:

> *Salesperson:* It's been my experience that when people like you hear about "Life Care at Home," they want to confer with somebody about what they've found. Some people like to run the idea by their children, or they need to talk with their financial advisor or CPA about the financial implications of this.
>
> I'm curious, Mrs. Brown, who you think you might be talking with about "Life Care at Home?"
>
> *Mrs. Brown:* I'm certain I'll call my daughter in Seattle right away.
>
> *Salesperson:* Tell me about your daughter. What's her name and what kind of a person is she?
>
> *Mrs. Brown:* Her name is Monica. She's a very loving and protective mother and a faithful daughter. She works as a buyer for a large department store out there.
>
> *Salesperson:* She sounds like an exceptional person. You must be very proud of her.
>
> *Mrs. Brown:* I am. It's a joy to be her mother. She lives a long way away but she stays in touch as best she can.
>
> *Salesperson:* When you talk to her, what do you think you'll tell her about "Life Care at Home"?
>
> *Mrs. Brown:* I'll tell her that I've found the answer to my prayers, that now I'll be able to stay here in my home in Philadelphia, and everything will be well taken care of. I won't have to worry and neither will she.

Salesperson: And what kinds of questions do you think Monica will have about "Life Care at Home?"

Mrs. Brown: She'll want to know in detail what all they will do for me.

Salesperson: How will you answer that?

Mrs. Brown: I'll tell her that your organization will be like a master butler, making sure that all the details of running my household are looked after promptly and professionally. You'll also be like a communication center, keeping my family and friends informed and up to date on my situation. And you'll see that I get the best of personal care and medical care, around the clock if I need it.

Salesperson: It sounds like you have a pretty good handle on what our program is. What other questions will Monica have?

Mrs. Brown: For sure she'll want to know about the cost, and whether your company can be counted on down the road when I need help.

Salesperson: What will you tell her on those topics?

Mrs. Brown: I'll explain that there's a large down payment of $20,000 to get started, which is put in an annuity and held in escrow to guarantee the funds will be there when I start needing help, and there's a monthly payment of between a thousand and fifteen hundred dollars, depending on my current health status. I'll also tell her about your sponsoring organization, which she respects a lot.

Salesperson: That's a good explanation. What other comments do you think Monica will have?

Mrs. Brown: She may get into a discussion about how she was planning for me to come and live with her. She brings that up sometimes, but I think we both know it wouldn't work. She's got her hands full with children, a husband, and a job with lots of stress and responsibility. What in the world would she do with me underfoot?

Besides, I don't want to move way over there to the other side of the country. All my friends are here in Philadelphia, and this is home for me. All in all, arranging to stay in my own home is best for both her and me.

Salesperson: It sounds like you've thought through all of that before, Mrs. Brown. Thanks for sharing that with me.

I wonder who else you might be speaking to about this besides your daughter?

Mrs. Brown: For sure I'll need to talk to my financial advisor about what to cash in to make the down payment.

Salesperson: Would you mind telling me about your financial advisor?

Mrs. Brown: I work with Michael Thomas at Merrill Lynch. He was my husband's broker before my husband died and I just stayed on with him. He's mostly a numbers guy. I don't hear from him much unless he's pitching something.

Salesperson: What do you think he'll want to know from you about "Life Care at Home?"

Mrs. Brown: He'll want to know that it's a legitimate company and that I know what I'm doing with the money.

Salesperson: And do you know what you are going to say to him?

Mrs. Brown: Sure, I'll explain what you do, in the same way I described what I'd say to my daughter, and then I'll offer to send this brochure you gave me so he can check you out himself. He just wants to look like he's looking out for me as the widow of his long-time client.

Salesperson: It sounds like you're well prepared to talk to him.

Mrs. Brown: I think so.

The result of adding the Dress Rehearsal Story to their first meeting agenda was a dramatic turnaround in the number of cases closed, and a sharp decline in "Mr. Hydes" and "Tasmanian devils." For the company in Philadelphia and their sales team, it was the most valuable piece of the Double Your Sales process.

You should understand that the pure "dress rehearsal" version, as described in this story, is only one variation of The Dress Rehearsal Story, and in fact it is the most rigorous version. There are several other ways to accomplish this step, which I'll describe in the next section.

How Do You Use The Dress Rehearsal Story?

Your objective in The Dress Rehearsal Story is to engage the prospective customers' left brain after they have said "yes" or "maybe" and before they leave your presence. This can be accomplished in a variety of ways, most of which are simpler and less time consuming than the full-blown dress rehearsal dialogue.

The principle is to ask prospective customers what I call *"analysis-leading questions."* Just as a "story-leading question" is one that leads to the sharing of a story, an analysis-leading question is an inquiry that gets directed to left side of the brain and invites the respondent to analyze something.

Analysis-leading questions call for certain mental activities such as the following:

— Listing
— Ranking
— Summarizing
— Comparing
— Contrasting
— Outlining
— Numbering
— Explaining
— Calculating
— Questioning
— Reviewing

In other words, during this step of the Double Your Sales process you want to look for ways to encourage prospective customers to engage in left-brain thinking as they consider their decision to buy from you. Here are eleven more examples of how to it, in addition to the full-blown dress rehearsal described above.

1] Tell prospective customers that, because you covered a lot of ground in your meeting today, you would like to review and summarize the meeting together in order to make sure everyone is on the same page. Solicit their assistance in going through this review and summary.

2] Ask prospective customers what they think went well in your meeting and what still seems unsettled or unresolved.

3] Ask prospective customers how they see your products and services working to address the concerns they expressed in their Worry Story.

4] Ask prospective customers to list some of the advantages of purchasing your products or using your services.

5] Ask them to identify the three most important advantages to them.

6] Tell prospective customers you sometime lapse into technical jargon (such as "legalese") and you realize this may confuse people. As a way of confirming that you haven't confused them, ask if they will summarize the main points of your meeting in their own words *in plain English.*

7] Ask if they need information about your services or products in order to share it or explain it to a family member, friend, or advisor. Help prepare them to share information or answer questions.

8] If prospective customers are nervous or anxious about explaining their decision to someone else, offer to go with them or to talk to that other person yourself. Then get the prospective customers to prepare you for that conversation by thinking about questions the other person will have, their likely attitude, etc.

9] If they are inclined to "think about" your proposal, ask them to share with you their methodology for evaluating the advantages and disadvantages of what you offer.

10] In the case of prospective customers who have answered "maybe," ask them to picture that they are making a large chart on which they list "pros" on one side and "cons" on the other. Have them share with you what's on each side of the large chart.

11] Instead of an imaginary chart, help prospective customers who answered "maybe" to start a real "T diagram" chart on a sheet of paper they can take with them.

What Are Some Tips For Using The Dress Rehearsal Story?

The Dress Rehearsal Story is an excellent time to solidify the deal and to address any residual questions. I think it is important to invite prospective customers to share any concerns they may have about buying from you so you have a chance to address them yourself. This is the point in the process to extend that invitation.

I do not recommend, however, that your invitation be worded in such a way as to plant seeds of doubt where none exist. Unless your experience has taught you that a big concern always shows up after the meeting—in which case preemptively addressing it in the meeting may be the wise thing to do—you should stick to addressing prospective customers' actual concerns during this stage of the process. Don't put ideas in their heads. Don't ask for trouble by suggesting things they should worry about.

Besides solidifying the buying decision and addressing concerns, the Dress Rehearsal Story is also a good time to check on how well you communicated in the meeting. Here's an example of how to do that.

Some years ago, a widow I'll call Mrs. Green came to see me to amend a living trust drafted originally by someone else. In the course of getting to know her and her worries, it became pretty clear to me that the best solution for her situation was to create a charitable remainder trust.

(I don't usually diagnose problems and recommend solutions in the first meeting, but this situation seemed to call for that. She had come with a simple amendment in mind, but that was not the appropriate solution, so I needed to help her understand what the right solution was.)

Using an abundance of Hidden Waterfall Stories to make her aware of potential dangers and easily-missed opportunities, I was able to teach her what a charitable remainder trust was and to help her see the advantages of my recommendation. She had no hesitation when I quoted the fee and asked her if she was ready to go forward.

Because I wanted to make sure she clearly grasped what I had proposed, I asked if we could write out a list of the benefits that would come to her by using this particular solution. To my delight, the list came easily to her.

"Save capital gains taxes now. Save estate taxes later. Eliminate any confusion about my testamentary intent. Honor my deceased husband. Give support to the two churches where each of us grew up. Make a difference. Provide lifetime income for me. Give back to those causes my husband and I believe in. Give me peace of mind. Help me express gratitude for my blessed life."

I wrote the list on a yellow legal pad as she talked. When she ran out of things to add to the list, I turned the pad so she could see it and asked, "Mrs. Green, of all these benefits, which one is the most important to you personally?"

With tears in her eyes, she pointed to "Make a difference."

"That's the one," she said. "I want to know that my 'widow's mite' has in some small way made a difference in the world when I am gone."

I assured her that it would. And through The Dress Rehearsal Story, I was reassured that she understood clearly, both in her head and in her heart, the meaning and purpose of our work together.

How Do You Create The Dress Rehearsal Story?

There are lots of right ways to present The Dress Rehearsal Story to prospective customers. All who use the Double Your Sales process will find their own style and approach to this step, and they will likely have different versions of it for different prospective customers.

The two key questions in deciding which version of The Dress Rehearsal Story to use in a particular situation are "What feels comfortable to you?" and "What gets them to look at their decision from the analytical side of the brain?" Your own experience in selling your products and services will best inform your determination of how lightly or intensively you need to focus on this step of the process.

My recommendation is to experiment with different approaches until you find a few that fit your style best. They may be from the list of a dozen examples above, or you may discover your own.

Recognize that you will need to use different styles and approaches depending on the level of commitment and enthusiasm of the prospective customers. You would use a different approach with someone who is lukewarm and still "thinking about it," compared to someone who is excited and ready to get going.

Remember that you are not limited to one approach per meeting. It is sometimes more effective to use a combination of approaches with the same prospect. Notice that with Mrs. Green, I asked her to list benefits, and then I asked her to select the most important. This one-two punch created an ideal Dress Rehearsal Story for her.

Note that if you are speaking with several people, you may need to use a different approach with each of them, especially if each is in a different place with respect to the buying decision or if each has a different analytical/intuitive style.

How Do You Get Started Using The Dress Rehearsal Story?

I've found the best way to get started is to familiarize yourself with the dozen options I've listed above for implementing The Dress Rehearsal Story, and then to try one or two in each meeting with prospective customers. Stay open to trying several different approaches in different settings until you discover what works best for you.

Before long, you'll identify the approaches that feel most comfortable to you and that work with your prospective customers. If you remember that the purpose is to get Mr. Analytical to participate in the decision-making process while the prospective customers are still in your presence, you'll do just fine.

Chapter Summary

- The Dress Rehearsal Story is a technique for intentionally turning the meeting 'analytical" and speaking to the left side of the prospective customers' brain. The objective is to bring Mr. Analytical squarely into the conversation where you have an opportunity to influence his thinking.

- If your prospective customers say "yes" or "maybe" when you ask them to buy, you should initiate a discussion with them that engages their left brain. This will preemptively prevent Mr. Analytical from assaulting Mr. Intuitive's decision.

- Mr. Analytical will start questioning the decision sooner or later. You want that to be sooner, while Mr. Intuitive is still energized from what's gone on already in the sales meeting, and while you're there so you can participate in the conversation.

- The pure "dress rehearsal" version is only one variation of The Dress Rehearsal Story, and in fact it is the most rigorous version. There are several other shorter and simpler ways to accomplish this step.

- The principle is to ask prospective customers *"analysis-leading questions."* Just as a "story-leading question" is one which leads to the sharing of a story, an analysis-leading question is an inquiry that gets directed to the left side of the brain and invites the respondent to analyze. Analysis-leading questions call for certain mental activities such as listing, ranking, summarizing, or numbering.

- The two key questions in deciding which version of The Dress Rehearsal Story to use for particular prospective customers are "What feels comfortable to you?" and "What gets them to look at their decision from the analytical side of the brain?"

- You will use different styles of The Dress Rehearsal Story depending on the level of commitment and enthusiasm of the prospective customers.

- You are not limited to one approach per meeting. It is sometimes most effective to use a combination of approaches with the same prospect.

- Besides solidifying their buying decision and addressing any concerns your prospective customers have, the Dress Rehearsal Story is also a good time to check on how well you communicated in the meeting.

- To get started, familiarize yourself with the dozen options listed in this chapter, and then try them out until you discover what works best for you.

Chapter 17

The Next Step Story

Key Points

➤ The Next Step Story is a conversation and an agreement with prospective customers about what happens next in your relationship.

➤ The Next Step Story is low-tech and blatantly obvious, but unfortunately often overlooked.

➤ The Next Step Story makes sure, regardless of what decision prospective customers made—yes, no, or maybe—that everyone knows where you go from here.

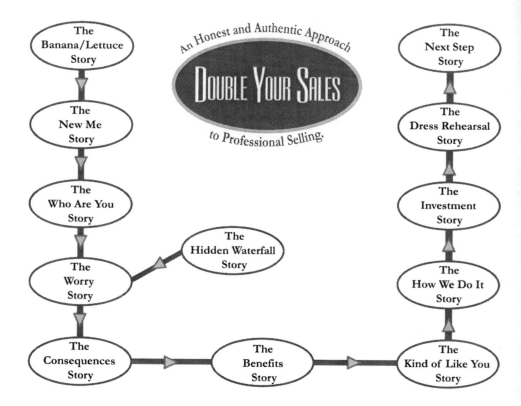

The Banana/Lettuce Story

The New Me Story

The Who Are You Story

The Worry Story

The Hidden Waterfall Story

The Consequences Story

The Benefits Story

The Kind of Like You Story

The How We Do It Story

The Investment Story

The Dress Rehearsal Story

The Next Step Story

An Honest and Authentic Approach

DOUBLE YOUR SALES

to Professional Selling.

What is The Next Step Story?

The Next Step Story is a conversation between you and the prospective customers in which you and they develop a clear picture and an agreement about how you will proceed from here. This is nothing fancy; in fact it is low-tech and blatantly obvious. Unfortunately, it is often overlooked.

What is the Purpose of The Next Step Story?

The purpose of The Next Step Story is to make sure everyone understands what will happen next in your relationship.

If the prospective customers agreed to buy your services or products, the purpose is to schedule and prepare for the next step in your customer process. You should take whatever action is appropriate to make sure they have a first-rate experience as your customer.

If they said no, the purpose is to determine what, if any, contact you will have with them in the future. If you see some future potential with them, you want permission to stay in touch, and you want to make sure you know what the best way is to do that. On the other hand, if future efforts are likely to be pointless, you should gently disengage.

If their answer is "maybe" or "not yet," the purpose of The Next Step Story is to explore how to help them get to "yes" in a way that is supportive and respectful to both of you. Reaching an understanding of what that looks like, and then securing permission to move forward based on that understanding, are the main objectives of The Next Step Story.

What is an Example of The Next Step Story?

What it sounds like depends on whether they've given you a "yes," a "no," or a "maybe." If it's a "yes," then here is an example of The Next Step Story:

> *Advisor:* I'm really looking forward to working with you. As you know from the diagram I made for you a few minutes ago, the next step in our process is the "Design Session." That will probably take about 90 minutes. If we can, I'd like to schedule that sometime next week. What does your schedule look like next week?

> *Husband:* I'm tied up on Tuesday, but I can make any other day work. I'd prefer not to do it on Friday, but if that's the only option, that would be OK. I'm anxious to get this done.

> *Wife:* Monday and Tuesday are out for me, but either Wednesday or Thursday afternoon would work.

> *Advisor:* In that case, let's make it Wednesday at 2 p.m., OK? Let's check with my assistant on the way out so she can get it on her calendar, and she has a list of information I'll need you to bring.

> *Husband:* Sounds great.

On the other hand, if they've given you a "no," it might look something like this.

> *Advisor:* I'm disappointed we won't be working together on this project, but I would like to stay in touch with you if that's alright. We send out a quarterly electronic newsletter to customers, contacts, and professional colleagues that is loaded with

useful ideas for how to maximize your investment results. Do you mind if I put you on our electronic mailing list?

Husband: That's OK as long as it's just quarterly. I get enough junk already in my inbox, so I don't need to be bombarded with a whole lot of stuff. But if it's not too frequent, I'd be curious about your thoughts about the market.

Agent: That sounds fair. I'll make sure you get the quarterly newsletter but we won't pester you with anything else. And thanks for coming in today. If your needs change, I hope you'll give me a call.

If their answer is "maybe" or "I need some time to think about it," then The Next Step Story might be more like this:

Advisor: I'm really glad we got to sit down together so I could learn about your needs and you could learn about my process for helping folks like you. I understand you need a little more time to determine if this is right for you. I recognize this is a big decision. You've shared with me a little bit about your personal decision-making process, and what I'd like to learn is how I can be most helpful to you as you're making this decision.

What I'd like to do, if it's OK with you, is to touch base with you next week to see if you have any further questions or if you need any additional information. Would that be alright with you?

Husband: I don't see why not, but I don't want to feel like I'm being pushed.

Advisor: I can assure you, I don't believe in being pushy, but I have learned that many people like you who need more time to think find they appreciate having a certain date to bring their thinking to a head. It helps them bring closure to their thought process. So what day next week could I check in with you?

Husband: Let's make it Friday.

Advisor: What's the best time on Friday?

Husband: 10:30 in the morning would be best for me.

Advisor: Great, I'll call you next Friday at 10:30 a.m. In the meantime, if you have any questions, feel free to call me.

How Do You Use The Next Step Story?

You use The Next Step Story to bring your sales meeting to a comfortable close and to create an understanding with prospective customers about what the future of your relationship will look like. If you've made a sale, you push your process forward. If they've turned you down, you explore what kind of relationship they want to have with you in the future. And if they're still deciding, you determine how you can follow up with them and hopefully move them to a "yes."

What Are Some Tips For Using The Next Step Story?

Whatever the prospective customers' decision, you should always seek to end the meeting having the ball in your court, that is, with permission for you to take the next action. This is especially important if their decision today is "maybe" or "we need to think about it."

If prospective customers will not give you permission to take the next step, that is often a strong negative indicator. In other words, if they say "maybe" or "we need more time to think about it," but they will not give you permission to follow up with them in some reasonable way, there is a strong likelihood their answer is really just a polite "no." Similarly, if they've said "no" and they aren't open to some form of ongoing "drip marketing," drop the matter—they aren't likely to become customers in the future.

On the positive side, if they've answered yes, The Next Step Story is a great opportunity to make sure the next part of your process is a smashing success. Help them understand and prepare for it, give them any materials that will assist them, and check to make sure no glitches can occur. Pave the way for a seamless transition from prospect to customer.

How Do You Create The Next Step Story?

You create The Next Step Story by picturing what you want to happen next (given the outcome of the meeting), describing what you are picturing, and then asking the prospective customers if your view is aligned with theirs. Make adjustments so your expectations and theirs are congruent. Make sure everyone is on the same page, and then document your next action. It's no more complicated than that.

How Do You Get Started Using The Next Step Story?

This is not rocket science. No special training or skills are required to start using The Next Step Story. It's just a matter of bringing up the issue at the end of each sales meeting, and then developing an agreement of what the story of your future relationship will look like.

So create a note, a checklist, or whatever type of mnemonic device works for you, so you don't forget to do it as you are winding down your meeting. In other words, just do it.

Chapter Summary

- The Next Step Story is simply reaching an understanding with the prospective customers about what happens next in your relationship.

- The Next Step Story should be simple and straightforward, moving those who have said "yes" forward in your process, setting up those who have said "no" for any future contacts they are willing to receive, and positioning yourself to have a positive influence on those who answered "maybe."

- An unwillingness to work with you regarding future contacts or to set up an opportunity for you to "check back with" them in the case of a "maybe" is often a significant indicator there may not be much future here.

- Notwithstanding its simplicity and obviousness, it's vital you not skip or overlook this step. Doing so could unravel all your previous progress.

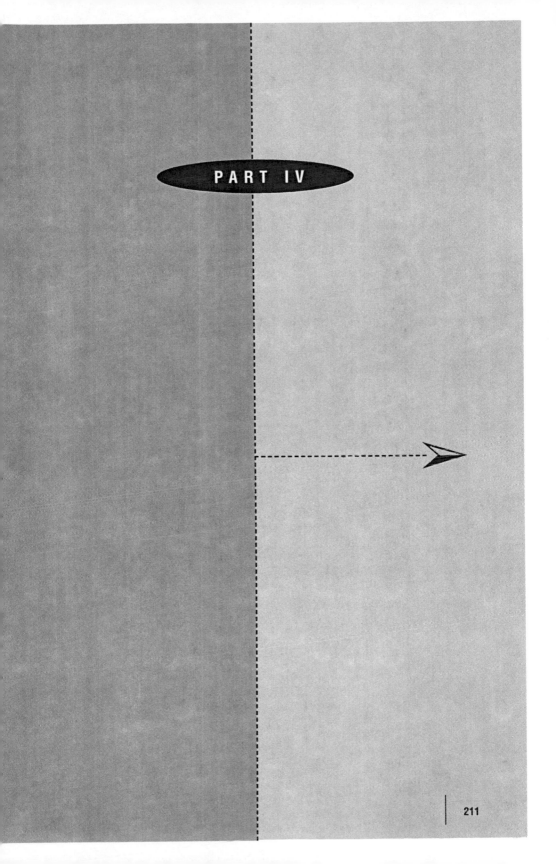

PART IV

Chapter 18

John's Discovery

The house was dark and everyone was asleep when John got home that night from the sales training course. His body and his brain were tired, but he didn't feel much like sleeping. He wished he could just disappear for a week while he tried to figure out what to do with his business and his life. ➤

There was a pile of mail for him on the desk by his computer. "More bills," he muttered to himself. "That's all I need right now."

But among the envelopes was a small parcel from Amazon. "That's funny," he thought, "I haven't ordered anything from them lately."

He checked the address. Sure enough, it was addressed to him.

Curious, he opened the package. It was a gift from Steve Wright, his best friend from college. Steve was always thoughtful and tried to stay in touch, but it wasn't like him to send books.

John looked at the book, *"Double Your Sales: An Honest and Authentic Approach to Professional Selling."* "Double your sales, huh?" he said to himself. "I could sure use that. I wonder what Steve saw in this?"

John read Steve's note:

"Dear John, I heard through the grapevine that you were having difficulty turning prospects into clients and were looking for help. This book has totally turned my business around and I'm guessing it might be exactly what you need right now. I think it'll be right up your alley. Friends forever, Steve"

John turned the book over and reviewed the back cover. "Impressive testimonials," he thought. "From 45% to 90%? Eighteen in a row? And even doctors can do this? Maybe Steve's on to something here."

John opened to the Introduction. "Simple and obvious. Hmmm. And it works?" He was curious. He settled into his chair and started to read.

"Well, sure, that makes sense."

"He's right, that *is* pretty obvious."

"Hey, I knew that. Wonder why no one ever said it like that before?"

"I love the diagram. Makes it easy to follow."

"I think I can do this."

"Wow, that's exactly what happened to me."

"I *really* think I can do this."

The pages flew by. When John paused to look up at the clock, it was long past midnight and he was more than halfway through the book. His body was tired, but his mind was racing, making plans for his upcoming prospect meetings.

"It all makes sense now," he thought. "I can see where I was messing up, and I understand why the program I just attended won't work for me. It's not who I am or how I operate. But this approach, this is how I want to treat my prospects so they become my clients. Steve said this turned around his business. I think it will do the same for me."

Now that he knew where to find the answer about what to do next, John could finally relax and go to bed. He was exhausted but very encouraged. "I'll finish the book in the morning and then go online and find out how to get more training. This is definitely what I was looking for."

John slipped into bed, kissed his wife gently so as not to wake her, and turned over.

"Thanks, Steve," he whispered. "Friends forever indeed."

Chapter 19

What's Your Next Step?

As you've learned already, The Double Your Sales process is a 12-step program for professionals who are sick and tired of losing sales. It's a proven remedy for those seeking to recover from poor sales results. It's powerful medicine for salespeople who want to boost their business by being themselves, telling the truth, and helping customers address their real concerns. ➤

The Double Your Sales process is not for everyone. It's not for those who believe a salesperson can't be honest and authentic and still "close the deal"; who believe customers must be pressured by artificial urgency; or who believe they already know all there is to know about selling.

But since you've read this far in the book, odds are that the Double Your Sales process *is* right for you, that it makes sense to you, and that you're considering how to put it to work for you.

If that's the case and you'd like more help, let me invite you to take the next step. My company, SunBridge, teaches professionals how to implement the Double Your Sales process in their work with prospective customers. We offer three convenient training alternatives:

The live, on-site, intensive two-day *Double Your Sales Professional Seminar* is for those who want the best possible experience as they learn this process, and who are looking for the quickest and most effective path to implementation. The Seminar is taught by me personally or by another seasoned master of the Double Your Sales process. The Seminar consists of instruction, examples, exercises, activities, rehearsals, and interaction that will absolutely have you using the process with skill and confidence at the end of two days. It includes, at no additional cost, a two-month group coaching module by live telephone conference calls to help you stay on track, follow up after the Seminar, and fully implement the Double Your Sales process in your business.

A self-study training program on audio CDs and workbook, *Double Your Sales Self-Study System,* is for professionals who like to get their training at their own pace in their own place. It includes written assignments and worksheets to make the Double Your Sales process immediately a part of your customer engagement system. The program includes, at no additional cost, a two-month group coaching module by live conference calls to follow up and support your implementation of the process.

The **Double Your Sales Customized Group Workshop** is for organizations that want us to create and present a customized, dedicated seminar to their sales professionals. In addition to all the benefits of the live, intensive Double Your Sales Professional Seminar, as noted above, this format allows us to focus on specific issues and unique situations faced by your group. In addition, a customized follow-up and implementation program will ensure that all participants successfully implement the training they receive in the workshop.

You can learn more about these options and order or sign up for our training, services, and products by visiting our website at *www.DoubleYourSalesNow.com.*

If you want to discuss Double Your Sales training for a group, or you're interested in intensive one-to-one coaching with this process, please email us at *admin@DoubleYourSalesNow.com* or call us at 407-593-2386. We'll be happy to talk about how we can help you, a small group of professionals, or your entire sales organization become masters of this powerful process.

So now the ball is in your court. If you're ready for an honest and authentic approach to professional selling, and you're ready for more prospects and bigger sales, we'd love to help.

Scott Farnsworth
President and Founder
SunBridge, Inc.
3214 Bayflower Avenue
Harmony, Florida 34773
Telephone 407-593-2386
Fax 407-292-6242
scott@DoubleYourSalesNow.com
www.DoubleYourSalesNow.com

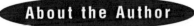

Scott Farnsworth is an attorney and a Certified Financial Planner©. He is the president of SunBridge, Inc. and the founder of The Legacy Builder Network. This is his third book. He is the author of *Closing the Gap: A Revolutionary Approach to Client Services,* and *Like a Library Burning: Sharing and Saving a Lifetime of Stories.*

Scott was recently named one of *Financial Advisor Magazine's* "Innovators of the Year." He designs and delivers transformative workshops for professionals, including *"The Legacy Builder Retreat," "Mastering the High End Close," "The Double Your Sales Professional Seminar"* and *"The Wealth & Wisdom Summit."* He is the inventor of The SunBridge Money & Success Client Connection System™, and is a certified Time to Think® Facilitator, Coach and Consultant.

Scott is a native of Fruitland, New Mexico. He earned his undergraduate degree *magna cum laude* in Portuguese and Political Science and his law degree *magna cum laude* at Brigham Young University. During law school he was the Managing Editor of the Law Review, and he published two scholarly articles. Following graduation, he was appointed Judicial Clerk for Paul H. Roney, Circuit Judge for the United States Court of Appeals for the Fifth Circuit.

He has nearly three decades of professional experience as an estate-planning attorney and financial planner, was Vice President and Trust Officer at Trustmark National Bank, and was an assistant professor of business law at the University of Southern Mississippi. He and his wife Marcie live in Harmony, Florida, and have six children and five grandchildren.

To contact Scott, please call 407-593-2386 or visit *www.DoubleYourSalesNow.com.*

Dedication

This book is dedicated to three extraordinary, angelic women without whom it would never have seen the light of day.

The first and by far the most important is my wife, Marcie Farnsworth. She is my confidante, my best friend, and my eternal soul mate. I was smitten the first minute I laid eyes on her and heard her speak, and have remained so throughout the third of a century we've shared since. She embodies a rare combination of compassion, intelligence, charm, and clear-eyed practicality, and is my most insightful counselor. Building a life together with her and our six remarkable children has been an absolute joy for me. Her unwavering support has made writing this book possible.

I am deeply grateful to my dear friend and colleague Nancy Kline. I have been deeply affected by her work at Time to Think and her vision of turning the whole world into a Thinking Environment®. She has taught me to think more courageously, to listen more attentively, and to appreciate more deeply, three attributes she personifies. Without her influence and encouragement and the thinking that emerged as a result, this book would never have been written.

I am equally grateful to Sharon Greenway, SunBridge's invaluable Director of Operations, for her drive, diligence, and hard work. I am constantly amazed and blessed by her willingness to dive in and learn new skills whenever required by our joint projects. Her tireless energy and brilliant creativity make me look good and have given me the time and space I needed to focus on this book. Her friendship and enthusiasm have made working together a true delight.

Breinigsville, PA USA
24 February 2010
233062BV00003B/2/P